Catch the Spark within

Transform a mere existence into a joy-filled authentic life.

ALEX ABAZ

DEDICATION

"Catch the Spark Within" is dedicated to my son Brad for all the joy
and laughter he has sparked in me.

CONTENTS

     unwelcome.

35   Weddings are beautiful.   98

36   Holidays are dessert.   103

37   I discovered thrift stores way too late.   105

38   Dance is about connectedness and relationships are a dance. 109

39   Celebrations are the highlights of our lives.   112

40   Live, laugh, and just be.   116

     References & Quotations   118

     About the Author   122

     Other Books by Alex Abaz   123

PREFACE

*Everyone has the spark of the
Divine within. When that spark is
alit by the hidden awe of the
everyday, which we take for
granted, a miserable existence
becomes a joy-filled and authentic
life. – Josie Aberdeen*

-

We are each a thread in the cosmic quilt. And like a thread, it is the twists and turns in our lives which contribute to the universal design. Many people today live lives that are frayed and fragile because they have followed the beat of a drum - perhaps social, perhaps familial - which often times are not in sync with the beat of their own heart.

The natural phenomenon of a belly laugh that brings tears to the eyes and cleansing to the soul are few and far between. The spark within is almost out.

New days are faced with dread. There is a gnashing of teeth and a panic and fear of what new terror lurks at the door. The spark within is almost out.

The threads of our lives are coming undone and we feel powerless to stop it.

But all of this is an illusion - the seeming powerlessness, the fears, the panic, the angst and agonies - the terror. The spark within has never died. All it ever needs is a bit of breeze to fan it into a life.

ACNOWLEDGEMENTS

The spark in my life is lit up by a circle of family and friends. Their love and continuous support invigorates me and fans my joy. I am grateful to my friend and coach Josie Aberdeen, a staunch supporter who's been encouraging me to do what I love.

1 | UNLOCKING THE FULLNESS OF LIFE.

What is the secret to happiness? For me, it is the practice of focusing on what is good in our lives. It is finding joy in the ordinary. It is pondering what is essential for our happiness. One way to train ourselves to do this is to read inspirational verses and keep a gratitude journal. This simple distraction can pay huge dividends.

A gratitude journal puts us on a path of inspiration through active meditation. It leads us to still waters. By sifting out what really matters we are motivated to improve our circumstances. When we immerse ourselves in positive light, we shine. The secret is to live gratefully, laugh often, and just be. Be who you are. Be where you are

– in the moment. I found that this process helped me through some challenging days and traumatic events. As it happens, when life hurts the most, it is most difficult to do anything. That's because the energy flow within us gets blocked. Shock and pain can do that to one's consciousness. But this is when this practice is most therapeutic.

As a stay-at-home mom, working full time from home, my experiences are mostly mundane. Sometimes they are chaotic and occasionally adventurous. You may identify with that. Life stressors can deplete our energy. Relationship and financial issues can cripple us. I started a gratitude journal at a time when there was some distress in my life. Active meditation kept me sane during the worst of it and sustained me to the next day. I made it a point of writing at least five things that I was grateful for each day. This practice required that I look for blessings throughout my day. That changed my focus and my attitude. Some days it was hard to find even one thing to praise. Repetition was unavoidable but that's not necessarily a bad thing. The inner spirit is comforted by rhythm and chant. Our subconscious does not mind repetition – it approves of it. This is how change happens. There were days when I was too busy or in shock and found it impossible to journal. That's okay too.

Most of us 'live' in a virtual reality of theatre and fantasy. We are led to believe that everyone but us is living a fantastical life. The lifestyle of the 'rich and famous' is alluring. It raises our expectations and desires only to give way to disappointment. Reality doesn't always have a happy ending. There were trials and tribulations during that season which changed my life forever. A path of inspiration and gratitude, while seemingly elementary and simple to follow, can be life-altering. It teaches us to focus on the positive in our lives, no matter how insignificant it may seem. In this way the negative is automatically diminished. This helps us cope with our circumstances and leads us to a more beautiful place, where we can experience joy and tranquility despite it all. According to Dr. Daniel G. Amen, author of "Magnificent Mind at any Age: Natural Ways to Unleash Your Brain's Maximum Potential", research has shown that those who wrote down five blessings each day and meditated on them throughout the day were happier within three weeks.

Each day presents us opportunities to learn from, and scattered here and there, we get snippets of joy and delight. By meditating on blessings throughout the day we heal ourselves. When we connect to the divine we are infused with good feelings and a sense of harmony, even in the midst of chaos. Meditation makes the brain wakeful and relaxed – ready to process. By editing the imagery that reaches our brain we modulate our feelings. There is always beauty on our path if we train our eye to look for it. In beauty there is awe. Its breath first snares us and then releases us, but by then we've experienced wonder, inspiration, and abandonment.

A grateful heart makes our spirit soar. We're brimming with happiness. Our cup runs over with goodness and kindness. Living in the moment really does make us happier. Life cannot sparkle when we're not fully present and ready to catch all the sparks. Being ready means that we know who we are and what really matters to us. Only then can we be true to ourselves. A prism can catch and release light because it's transparent. "Know thyself" are words ascribed to Socrates. It's ancient wisdom and a magic cure for a depleted spirit. Often times we lose ourselves. That happens when we're moving too fast or when we avoid being who we are. When we're not grounded in what *is*, our perception plays tricks with our minds. We convince ourselves that we're not enough or that we don't have enough. It's a negative spiral. Not questioning leaves us vulnerable. Unknowingly we can live a lie and it becomes who we are. The disguise is most convincing. Revealing ourselves can be scary. Most of us find it difficult to accept let alone divulge our inner truth. It's too raw. But something cries out to us and we want to discover who we really are. What are we all about? When we are willing to be honest everything falls into place somehow. Truth sets the human spirit free. We are only happy when we are truly ourselves. It's quite amazing really. We can only be who we are and it's the only way that we fit into the world.

Life is a *live* performance. We have to be awake so we don't miss any of it. Sleepwalking through it cuts us out of our own script. We look but cannot see. But it's not enough to be a spectator. We have to participate to feel the joy of triumph. Confidence comes from knowing and doing. When we're confident we walk tall. We don't wobble. Our self-worth is transparent and we get the respect we deserve. That's because we're genuine and are willing to share in a non-threatening kind of way. We don't sweat the small stuff. The sparkle of life is so bright that it captivates us. We expect good things to happen and anticipate them with a ready spirit. When we raise our standards and believe we can achieve them, we become everything we aspire to being. That's because we stop sabotaging ourselves. Once we figure out who we are and what we want, we get going. We notice what is or is not working for us and change our approach. Our GPS is set to our destination so we don't have to worry about how to get there. We don't let any of the distractions blind us. Our EGO is dismissed so we are not tied to the outcome. Success doesn't come at the end – by then the show is over. There's good reason to celebrate beginning and every step after that. As a spectator we are applauding every thrill we get from the performance.

Life is a gift not to be squandered. Regret is not a coupon which we can redeem. I hope that by unlocking the fullness of life through active meditation you find the courage to persevere no matter what circumstances you face. Life offers us lots of choices. We have to choose at every crossroad – life doesn't wait. There is no right or wrong decision. It is only by looking back that we can tell what pivotal choices made the difference in the texture of our lives. The experience is all that matters. If we are willing to learn then we can avoid some bumps and enjoy a smoother ride. We have to have a willing spirit. Life is circular – it winds and loops back to the beginning. When we chase after life, it's a rollercoaster ride. You are exactly where you are supposed to be. Live, laugh, and just be. There is no reason to chase time, even if we could. All we can do is live each moment. Every moment is precious.

I am convinced that we are all addicted to optimism. We like to drown in happiness. Each blessing adds a pinch of happiness to your life. I hope you live your life in blissful tranquility. I hope you are inspired to be grateful every day. I wish you well on your journey of a lifetime.

2 | FRIENDS ARE ESSENTIAL.

Friends are not disposable. They are like oxygen. I am grateful for my best friend Cheryl. She's been there for me through thick and thin – a bosom friend indeed. Friendship is based on trust. It takes time to get to know people. Most of us hide inside a shell, afraid to show who we really are. Some try to blend into the world like chameleons. Others like to step out into the limelight. Don't let any of it fool you. It's all the same. We either sit back and hide in the crowd or jump up and get lost in our own performance. Ironically, honesty resonates with everyone but we avoid it because we assume we will be mocked and ridiculed. Sometimes we're suppressing emotions which are too painful for us to process. It takes courage to be who we are.

In the 2012 film, "A Thousand Words", Jack McCall (played by Eddie Murphy) is a literary agent who has the gift of the gab and boasts he can sell anything. When he stretches the truth to make a deal with a spiritual guru, Dr. Sinja (played by Cliff Curtis), he ends up with a Bhoji tree on his property which drops leaves with every word Jack speaks. Jack realizes that his fate is the same as that of the tree and believes that when all the leaves are gone he will die. He refrains from speaking which leads to problems in his marriage and his job in no time.

Dr. Sinja saw through Jack from the start and knows his antics are a cover-up for deep emotional wounds. When Dr. Sinja meets up with Jack again, his advice to Jack goes something like this, "It's quite amazing how many useless words one can speak. Don't you think? You don't look well Jack." Jack points to his ring finger, not wanting to waste his words. Dr. Sinja understands, "The marriage is over? She took the baby and left?" Jack taps a sheet of paper and Dr. Sinja says, "You lost your job too? Sorry Jack." Jack is annoyed and Dr. Sinja tells him, "All I have for you are my leaves and o' well, this toll bell from the airport." Jack cannot hold back, "God damn tree... undo it!" And Dr. Sinja tries to calm him down, "Please Jack. I know you're scared. I know I told you I'd come back with the answer. But the answer is ... 'there is no answer'. No one knows about the tree Jack. I tried... Ok? I don't know how it's going to work out for you but what I do know is that you need to find peace. [Jack is frustrated.] If you think I'm a sham, then why are you here? You want my advice? You need to find the truth about yourself. You need to get quiet Jack, not just with your mouth but with your mind and in that quiet you will hear the truth.

Do you have any other unresolved relationships in your life? [Jack holds back the truth and shakes his head.] Good. Good. Then your wife, does she know that you love her?" Jack blurts out, "I tell her all the time." Dr. Sinja replies, "Words. More words, Jack. You tell her, like losing those leaves that fly off a dying tree? Words... can't you show her that you love her. Make peace. Show them that you love them and be truthful. You need to accept the possibility that when all the leaves fall off that tree..." And Jack stops him from finishing the statement. After that Jack gets silent and then sets out to repair his relationships using up the few remaining leaves wisely. He visits his wife and tells her, "You...Me... Eternity."

Often we form an opinion about someone instantly. Before we know it, we've decided whether we like or dislike them after only a brief encounter. We are most comfortable with those people that closely reflect our own ideals and values, as we perceive them. They make it okay for us to be who we are. More often than not we get it wrong. I have changed my mind about people more than once. People I dismissed initially because I judged them to be difficult turned out to be quite easygoing, while others, whom I judged to be caring, turned out to be insensitive.

You have to be authentic to be a good friend. Mostly you have to be there. A friend is a confidant, a playmate, and a rescuer. My best friend is a comrade on a special outing and a comedian on an ordinary night. When she drops by, it's never an interruption. She's considerate and thoughtful. Sometimes she'll even bring the coffee. Lately a group of us has been getting together monthly for brunch – a buffet of calories and laughter. It's a lot of fun. I remember a time when young ladies sat together embroidering their trousseau. They'd laugh the afternoon away while they stitched colourful dreams on white-linen tapestries. It seems like a fairytale now.

Friendship is not a commodity to be bartered or played with. In the 2011 film "Black Gold", the Sultan Amar (played by Mark Strong) tells his son Prince Auda (played by Tahar Rahar), who's been sent to his father as an ambassador, "Nothing of value can be bought or sold." The Sultan is referring to an offer made by the Emir Nesib (played by Antonio Bandaras) to return his sons, Prince Auda and his brother, after 15 years of holding them hostage. They were taken as collateral to ensure that the Sultan kept out of the no man's land that lay between their two countries. The Emir now wants to exploit that no man's land and is bartering with gold and lives.

"Money can't buy back your youth when you're old, a friend when you're lonely, or peace to your soul," is how Jeff Buckley puts it in his song "Satisfied Mind". A friend is as precious as our youth and as satisfying as peace is to our soul. A life-long friend is an incredible blessing.

3 | IT IS BRAVE TO GO AFTER YOUR DREAMS.

We got to know Chris Rene in the first season of the talent show "The X Factor" in 2011. Prior to auditioning for the contest he was a trash collector. Chris is someone who went after his dream and inspired a nation. He captured our hearts with his authentic sensitivity and his triumph over alcohol and drug addiction. As a singer-songwriter he weaved his nightmares into songs. His song "Hey Young Homie" speaks about life as he knows it, "Hey, young homie what you trippin' on. Looking at life, like how did I get it wrong. Life's too short, gotta live it long." He told The X Factor audience, "This is your one life and you have to make it count." Old timers will ask you, "If not NOW, then when?" Regret is not a coupon that you can redeem.

We start out with many dreams but quickly walk away from them. Why is that? Like Dorothy in the 1939 film "The Wizard of Oz", we wish to meet the Wizard and ask him to make our dreams come true. But most of us never even set out on the yellow brick road. Sometimes we get distracted and other times we just lack the courage or clarity to follow the path. We wait for a miracle. But true miracles are those we have a hand in. That's just what the Good Witch of the North told Dorothy. She never needed the Wizard to send her back home. You can dream it, but if it doesn't materialize, it's like it never was. Those who risk – win. The salmon braves strong currents, jumps over hurdles, and leaps over boulders to swim upstream to mate. It is genetically driven to do this when it's time. The salmon is on a mission. We need to translate our dreams into missions with goals and timelines. If salmon can do it, so can we.

"Happiness is not the pursuit of pleasure. It's the pursuit of *necessariness...* We are hard-wired to seek out unshakeable meaning," says Arianna Huffington. She's talking about our need to discover our purpose in life. Ever since I can remember, I've been on a quest to find meaning. When I was young I had dreams of becoming this and that. My vision was a blurred outline which lacked specificity. Perhaps that was because what I hoped to become was not what really mattered. I was after the feeling of "being somebody".

There are times when we wimp out from pursuing our dreams. We want to believe but it seems impossible so we sabotage ourselves. One time I sang in a choir that performed in front of a large audience at Massey Hall in Toronto. It was a special night. I don't remember even telling my family about it so they didn't come to see me. I got a kick out of being on stage. In high-school I got a lead role in a play. My sister Beth worked all day and all night to sew two beautiful baroque dresses, one for me and another for someone else's part. It was a labour of love that endeared her to me forever. The feeling I got on stage swept me away but that was my last brush with fame. It's brave to be a non conformist. I lacked the courage and confidence to follow my passions. If we don't believe in our dreams they won't happen.

In the 2011 film "One Day", Dexter (played by Jim Sturgess) and Emma (played by Anne Hathaway) are best friends. In the "15th of July, 1991" scene, Emma is frustrated with her job. She's been waitressing in a Mexican eatery for two years, a place she called "the graveyard of ambition". Emma has some news for Dexter, "I got offered the job as manager today. They told me they wanted someone who wasn't going anywhere." Dexter is irritated, "Alright Em. Listen. I think you should take a bottle of Tequila. I think you should walk out the door and I don't think you need ever come back." Emma is stuck, "But my job is my life," and Dexter counsels her, "You can't throw away years of your life just because... what? You think it's funny," and Emma disgusted with herself says, "My hair smells of cheese...Monterey Jack cheese." Dexter continues, "Look. I thought you were writing poetry," and Emma explains, "No. Go where the money is. Tried that. Failed." Dexter follows

Emma around while she raises the chairs onto the tables and says to her, "Look. You just can't see it. Can you? You're funny. You're attractive. You're smart. You're the smartest person I know," but Emma is not convinced, "Sure," and Dexter tells her, "You are. You're attractive. You're sexy." Emma does not buy it, "What," and Dexter says, "What? Is that supposed to be sexist or something?" Emma clarifies, "No. It's not sexist. It's just ridiculous."

Dexter walks over and puts his arms tightly around her shoulders, "Em listen... if I could just give you one gift, ah one gift for the rest of your life, you know what I'd give you? Confidence. It's either that or a scented candle." He kisses her forehead. Their tête-à-tête is interrupted by Ian (played by Rafe Spall) who's got a crush on Emma, "Emma... so I've disinfected the meat fridge," and Emma thanks Ian, "My hero. Thank you, Ian. See you tomorrow." Ian is brushed off by Dexter, "Bye mate," and Ian says, "Bye Emma." Emma is exhausted with her life, "I should go too," and Dexter says, "All right," and Emma adds, "I'll be fine. I'm just... Ohhh... I feel a bit lost. That's all." Dexter tells her, "Everyone is lost at 25," and Emma argues, "You're not. Trainee TV producer. Nice new flat. CD player. Group sex on Tuesdays and Fridays." But Dexter knowingly says, "Well, you know.. I'm crying on the inside." They have a shot of Tequila and Dexter says to Emma, "You know what you need, don't you? ... You need a holiday."

After we lose our way, we forget our passions. Life without passion is flat – it's lethargic. So how can we unearth our passions again? That which we admire is a clue. Notice what you like to watch on TV or read on the Web, the subjects that you find interesting, that which amuses you, the kind of people you respect. What is it that you admire most about them? What do you care about most in the world? Something that you find embarrassing to do can be a clue to a buried passion. If you get swept away or immersed in something without being conscious of time passing, you're in your element. Find the anecdotal evidence about "what is missing in your life'. In the 2003 film "Under the Tuscan Sun", Frances Mayes writes, "Life offers you a thousand chances ... all you have to do is take one." Don't sell out your dreams. Don't wait for a wizard or a miracle. Be brave. Live them.

4 | FLEXIBILITY IS AN ELASTIC FIBER THAT STRETCHES LIFE.

Flex-ability can turn a chore into an excursion, a challenge into an opportunity, and a minute into a memory. A rigid lifestyle is an obsession which stifles creativity and growth. In life we have to be most flexible with our attitude.

Most of the time we are in a hurry and want to get where we are going without detours. Traffic lights slow us down. The idea that we may be late to our destination is irritating. Our chores and obligations are numerous and we're anxious to get them done in record time. We can't possibly squeeze fun into the mix! Do you not get a laugh from watching someone weaving, tailing, and making erratic lane changes trying to get wherever faster, only to meet up with them at the next stop? They are chasing time! What if we decided to take the less-travelled side roads and skip the well-travelled route with all its congestion and traffic jams? How about mixing up the chores? We could change the order or the time when we set out, for example. Would it help if we made a pit stop at one of our favorite places where we could just sit, gawk, and be amused for a while? What if we played a game along the route like I Spy? If we would just settle down and accept the commute, we might enjoy the journey. We may actually be charmed by something new along the way.

Sometimes we have the time but lack the will. We are set in our ways and prefer that things didn't change. We have a routine that we follow on week-days and week-ends. It is how we've done it in the past and how we intend to keep doing it. Doing the same thing day in and day out is reassuring. But while it may be easy to keep doing it the same way it doesn't allow for discovery or growth. A lifestyle that is way too predictable is dull. An inflexible attitude does not accept deviation, consultation, or compromise. It makes it hard to be in a relationship. A rigid personality will not lean towards another or embrace a different point of view. When our stiffness becomes an obsession, we lose our ability to cope or adapt to unexpected events which do happen. It may be hard to stretch but it's necessary.

Obsessions make for great drama. In the 2010 film "Charlie St. Cloud", Charlie (played by Zac Efron) loses his brother Sam (Charlie Tahan) in a horrible car accident. Charlie also "dies" on the scene but is revived by a paramedic who does not believe "in lost causes". Charlie and Sam were very close – they were inseparable. Sam looked up to his big brother who was also a substitute father. When the film starts, we see Charlie and Sam racing a sailboat, the Splendid Splinter, and win. We learn that Charlie is an avid sailor and he's unbeatable. Tess (played by Amanda Crew) came third in the race. She seems to have an interest in Charlie, although he doesn't seem to notice her. It's almost graduation and Charlie is supposed to attend Stanford University in the fall on a sailing scholarship.

Before the accident, Charlie promises Sam that they will practice baseball together every day until he leaves for Stanford. They were to meet punctually at sunset when the "Bailey's Yacht Club" ceremonial cannons sounded. Sam says to Charlie, "Promise, through rain or shine, hell or high water," and Charlie says, "I promise." After the funeral, Charlie is broken-hearted and runs into the woods where he sees Sam and they play catch. Charlie reaffirms his promise to his brother. Five years later Charlie is the full-time caretaker of the cemetery. He is living in a one-room cottage on the grounds. He meets Sam every day at sunset, in the canyon, after the sounding of the cannons.

Charlie is known in town for his oddness; "The St. Cloud kid is certifiable," they say. When Tess comes on the scene again, she is a about to set out on a six-month sail around the world. She and Charlie connect, and in a twist of events, spend the night together. The problem is that Charlie cannot tear himself away from the daily ritual he has with Sam. Charlie tells Tess that the more he is in her world, the less he can be in Sam's. Later, Charlie discovers that Tess went missing during a storm, three days earlier. Now Charlie must choose between saving Tess or keeping his appointment with Sam. Charlie chooses to save Tess' life and breaks the spell. He buys a boat and he and Tess sail around the world together.

It is laudable to want to keep a promise that is not a made-up obsession. It is also reasonable to rethink a decision when there is a solid argument against it. We all like to say "if you don't bend you'll break" and we do mean "you". The truth is that most of us like things our way and are firmly convinced our way is the right way. The fallacy of this claim is clear when we look at life through our rear-view mirror.

Be flexible. Take a different route whenever possible. It may be frustrating to navigate unknown routes but man has been exploring for millennium. The usual route can become interesting when you pay attention to the detail – the landscape, the architecture, the awnings, the people... Look at your surroundings and discover them all over again. It's transformative. Weave fun into the fabric of everyday living. It will reward you with double the pleasure.

5 | SERENDIPITY IS WHAT HAPPENS WHEN YOU STRAY OFF THE BEATEN PATH.

I chanced upon the storybook "Serendipity" by Stephen Cosgrove, an allegory about a sea monster who fights pollution to protect the sea creatures. I was scintillated by the theme as much as my child was captivated by the mythical creatures. Serendipity is hatched without a name but is later given her name by a walrus and a dolphin, who are the King and Queen of all the fishes even though they are not fishes, after the sea monster rescues the dolphin and gets rid of pollution. I was left dumbfounded. The way of Serendipity held such promise. If one believes then wisdom, purpose, and good deeds are to be found by straying off the beaten path.

The word "serendipity" was invented by Horace Walpole at the end of the 18th century to describe what happened in the fairytale "The Three Princes of Serendip" (now Sri Lanka). "In ancient times there existed in the country of Serendippo, in the Far East, a great and powerful king by the name of Giaffer. He had three sons who were very dear to him. And being a good father and very concerned about their education, he decided that he had to leave them endowed not only with great power, but also with all kinds of virtues of which princes are particularly in need." He entrusts their education to the best tutors but fears that his sons are too sheltered and privileged. The loving father offers each son the throne and when they refuse, in sham anger sends them away from the land." They decide to travel as common men rather than princes, "As their highnesses travelled, they were always making discoveries, by accident and sagacity, of things they were not in quest of." (Richard Boyle @2000). The fairytale is the English version of "Peregrinaggio di tre giovani figlioli del re di Serendippo" published by Michele Tramezzino in Venice (1557) based on folklore about the life of Persian King Bahram V who ruled the Sassanid Empire (420–440). Horace Walpole coined the word based on his recollection of the "silly fairytale" where the three princes by "accident and sagacity" discern the nature of a lost camel and win the favor of the Emperor, who spares their lives, lavishes them with riches, and makes them his advisors.

Do you believe in serendipity? Finding a "jewel of something" when you're not expecting it. That something may be an opportunity, a guide, a friend, cash, joy, or anything else that you weren't seeking but will make your life easier or better. It's a happy surprise! It's an offering from the universe that knows what you need before you even do and puts it on your path so you may find it. Serendipity is about Devine intervention in our destiny. Some call it fate. Whenever we set out on "paths untrodden" we see an invisible hand at play. Dorothy (played by Judy Garland) in the 1939 film "The Wizard of Oz", sets out to The Emerald City to find the Wizard to help her get back home. While travelling on the yellow brick road she meets a Scarecrow, a Tin Man, and a Cowardly Lion who are in need of a brain, a heart, and courage and decide to accompany her to ask the Wizard for these qualities. As it happens, they discover along the way that they already have these qualities and Dorothy always had the power to return home but needed to find this out for herself. But they needed each other to make the discovery.

Do we control our own destiny or is there an all-powerful force in charge? In the 2011 film, "The Adjustment Bureau", agents of fate make all the "big decisions" in people's lives. We are told that we are allowed to make the trivial ones for our amusement. The Chairman of this Bureau has written "a plan" for Elise Sellas (played by Emily Blunt), a beautiful contemporary ballerina with a bright future ahead of her. David Norris (played by Matt Damon), an ambitious young politician, has just lost the race for the New York Senate in a last-minute glitch. He's in the men's bathroom when Elise comes out of a booth and explains, "Sorry about that. I didn't mean to eavesdrop. I just didn't know what to do. Because I heard you come in and say hello and I probably should have said hi ... thought that would be weird, 'cause it's the men's. Um.. and then you started talking to yourself and.. and it was obviously very personal, so I was kinda stuck in no man's land…it all got to be too much, so I came out." David and Elise start talking and connect instantly but he is pulled away to give his speech.

David bumps into Elise on the bus while commuting to a new job. She writes her telephone number on a card for him before getting off. When David arrives at his workplace he is apprehended by a group of thugs with hats. Richardson (played by John Slattery) says to David, "You've just seen behind a curtain that you weren't even supposed to know existed. It must be jarring. It's not your fault … you were supposed to spill your coffee as you entered the park this morning … you would have missed the bus, and you would have arrived at work ten minutes later than you did and we would have been gone." Richardson explains, "We call that an adjustment. See sometimes when people spill their coffee … it's chance … sometimes it's us nudging people back on plan … when nudging isn't enough, management authorizes a recalibration. We deploy our intervention team and they change your mind for you …Very few humans have seen what you've seen today. And we're determined to keep it that way. So, if you ever reveal our existence, we'll erase your brain. The intervention team will reset you. Your emotions, your memories, your entire personality will be expunged … Okay. Oh, one more thing … you bumped into a woman this morning on the bus, Elise," and David asks, "What…what has that to do with anything?" Richardson tells him, "Well, you were never supposed to see her again," and David asks, "What is…what does that matter?" Richardson goes on, "Because it matters." They grab David's wallet, pull out the card with Elise's telephone number and light it up. Apparently David and Elise are not destined to be together. She is to marry her boyfriend and he is to win elections and get to higher places. That's the plan.

The film is about how David stumbles along over the next four years trying to be with Elise contrary to the plan. When Harry Mitchell (played by Anthony Mackie), an agent with a conscience, sees David scribbling combinations of telephone numbers, he tries to persuade David to give up Elise and explains how The Adjustment Bureau works. David asks, "… what were they doin' to Charlie?" And Harry says, "Just changin' the way he weighs investment risks, which subtly shift the direction of his company in the way upstairs wants." Next David asks, "So Richardson can read my mind," and Harry answers, "Richardson was tryin' to scare you," and David says, "No, he knew the number I was thinking of, the color." Harry explains, "Because he set it up as a choice. Choose a color, choose a number? We can't read your mind or hear your thoughts ..." David is curious about Harry, "Are you an angel," and Harry answers, "We've been called that ... more like case officers." Harry tells David to forget this girl and move on but David is not swayed.

The Bureau puts many roadblocks in front of David, "Wow, the ripples must just be endless. I don't care what you put in my way, I'm not givin' up!" But the Bureau is determined not to fail. When small roadblocks are not effective, the case is escalated to Thompson (played by Terence Stamp) who explains to David about free will and how we keep messing things up whenever we have it. Thompson says, "You have free will over which tooth paste you use .... But humanity just isn't mature enough to control the important things." David argues, "So you handle the important things? Well, the last time I checked the world's a pretty screwed up place," and Thompson says, "It's still here. If we'd left things in your hands it wouldn't be."

Thompson tries to dissuade David from seeing Elise. He appeals to David's ambition and his obligations to his dead father and brother. When that doesn't work, he plays the guilt card, "If you stay with her, it not only kills your dreams, it kills hers..." When Elise hurts her ankle, and Thompson appears to be responsible, David abandons Elise. Eleven months later when he learns that she's getting married, he decides he can't give her up and asks Harry to help him get to her. David convinces Elise to forgive him for hurting her and to trust him, "Okay, I can go through this door alone. You'll never see me or the people chasing us again. Or you can come with me, and I don't know what's on the other side, but I'd know you'd be next to me. And that's all I wanted since the minute I met you." And Elise says, "I'm coming with you." They end up at the top of the building of the Bureau headquarters surrounded. Thompson approaches them, "Did you really think you could reach The Chairman? And change your fate if you did? Or write your own? It doesn't work like that. And I told you why?" Then Harry hands Thompson a letter, "I've got a message for you," and Thompson reads the message, and says, "I understand." He looks at David and Elise and then quietly walks away. Harry says, "Even Thompson has a boss." David asks, "Harry? You're The Chairman," and Harry answers, "No! You've met him though, or her. Everybody has. The Chairman comes in a different form to everyone, so people rarely realize when it happens." David wonders, "Is this… some sort of test," and Harry answers, "In a way. It's all a test, for everybody … David, you risked everything for Elise. And Elise, when you came through that door at the Statue of Liberty, you risked everything too. But you inspired me. Seems like you inspired The Chairman too."

Referring to a paper in Harry's hand, David asks, "Is that about us? … What does it say," and Harry tells him, "It says that this situation between the two of you is a serious deviation from the plan. So The Chairman rewrote it…" David asks, "Okay. Now what," and Harry says, "Now… you can take the stairs." He takes his "magic" hat back and walks away from them. We hear a voice over of Harry summing everything up, "Most people live life on the path we set for them. Too afraid to explore any other. But once in a while people like you come along and knock down all the obstacles we put in your way. People who realize free will is a gift, you'll never know how to use until you fight for it. I think that's The Chairman's real plan. And maybe, one day, we won't write the plan. You will."

Most of us are too afraid or too stubborn to tread onto new paths. If we do, we may be rewarded with a thrill or a nugget. Make the most of every outing. Add a short side-trip just for fun when you're out and about. You never know what you'll find. We are blind to the Divine hand that looks after us and the gifts that await us, but they are there for us nonetheless. It's serendipity! Our task is to stay committed. Believe!

6 | HARDSHIP AND POVERTY ARE AN ASSAULT ON ONE'S EXISTENCE.

"If you've ever been hungry, you'll never be full," is an old saying which I watched play out in my mother's own life. A child that grows up in hardship and poverty loses heart. They are robbed of the essence that makes the human spirit shine. Their self-worth, their confidence, and their fantasies are all buried. They may be vulnerable and constrained but they are not useless. My mother was a self-taught literate woman; she was courageous, hard-working, and in many ways ahead of her time. Poor people are very capable but without opportunity they are stuck. When one feels like they are between nowhere and not much else, their spirit is crushed. It's a waste of human capital.

In the 2012 film "The Hunger Games", Gale Hawthorne (played by Liam Hemsworth) startles Katniss Everdeen (played by Jennifer Lawrence) in the woods, as she's about to shoot a deer with her bow and arrow. Gale yells out, "What are you gonna do with that when you kill it," and Katniss shouts back, "Damn you, Gale! It's not funny!" Katniss and Gale are best friends living in the 12th District of Panam, a totalitarian nation set in a dystopian future. Gale asks Katniss, "What are you gonna do with a hundred pound deer, Katnap? It's Reaping Day, the place is crawling with Peacekeepers." Katniss answers, "I was gonna sell it, to Peacekeepers," and Gale says, "Of course you were." Katniss reproaches him, "Oh, like you don't sell to Peacekeepers," and Gale says, "No! Not today!" Katniss laments, "It was the first deer I've seen in a year. Now I have nothing." Gale throws a rock into a tree startling some birds and Katniss shoots her arrow at them and Gale says, "Okay."

Gale and Katniss find a spot to sit and talk about that which is most pressing on their minds – the reaping. Gale asks, "What if they did? Just one year. What if everyone just stopped watching," and Katniss answers, "But they won't, Gale." Gale insists, "What if they did? What if we did," but Katniss is realistic, "It won't happen." Gale goes on, "You root for your favorites, you cry when they get killed. It's sick," and Katniss agrees, "Yeah." Katniss is not too hopeful but Gale dreams of it, "We could do it, you know. Take off, live in the woods. It's what we do anyway," and Katniss says, "They'd catch us," and Gale answers, "Maybe." Katniss provides some gory detail, "Cut out our tongues or worse. We wouldn't make it five miles," but Gale boldly argues, "No, I'd get five miles, I'd go that way." Katniss reminds Gale, "I have Prim and you have your brothers," and Gale tells her, "They can come too." Katniss can't see it, "Prim in the woods," and Gale has to agree, "Well, maybe not." Katniss then says, "I'm never having kids," and Gale tells her, "I might. If I don't live here." And Katniss points out, "But you do live here," and Gale says, "I know. But if I didn't." Then Gale takes out the bread roll from his bag which he'd forgotten about and gives it to Katniss, and she exclaims, "Oh my God! Is this real?" Gale answers, "Yeah! It better be. It cost me a squirrel." Katniss splits the bread and shares it with Gale, and he says sarcastically, "Happy Hunger Games, and Katniss adds, "And may the odds be ever in your favor. How many times has your name entered it," and Gale answers, "Forty two. Guess the odds aren't exactly in my favor."

The futuristic analogy is not so far-fetched from our present-day situation. All the necessities which some take for granted are sparse or non-existent for others. A prosperous minority lives in comfort and luxury while the majority is deprived of basic needs. It's a meagre existence which forces the poor to navigate a labyrinth of constraints amid unrelenting pressure. It's sinful! Having to compromise on basic needs is damaging to the core. Not only does one suffer from not having their present needs met but they become so used to sacrificing, that they are forever enslaved by it. Even when circumstances change and they can afford more, they continue to act like they are poor. Poor people are discounted human beings.

We must understand our history to affect our future. We must cultivate a sense of respect for diversification and a desire for everyone to have the same opportunities as us. As the daughter of immigrants I felt the ridicule of my parent's ethnic accent, culture, and customs. When you are seen as a foreigner, people make assumptions about you. Ironically we are all foreigners in America except for aboriginal people. Ignorant people like to poke fun and make caricatures of immigrants (and anyone else who is discounted). I find it ironic that some people think that if you speak with an accent you know less than they do. People have similar aspirations and capacities everywhere in the world. We all cry from pain and laugh from joy. The difference between us and them lies only in the opportunities that we are given. None of us chose our nest or the country where we wished to be born. It's a lottery. Education and world travel teaches people to appreciate diversification. The mix is a good thing! An alloy is made stronger by adding different metals.

Arianna Huffington believes we have an instinctive longing for meaning and community and that we are all a mixture of good and evil but so far politicians have only appealed to our self-interest. She says that "we need to appeal to our better angel" and "not the devils of our worst nature". Her vision is of a caring and compassionate society which uses "creativity to fight fear and (the) little brain which is not rational." I listened to her being interviewed by Howard Fineman (Great Conversations #302) and she was inspiring. Impoverished nations need allies and growth strategies (development frameworks) if they are to help their people raise their standards of living. It is essential to provide education, healthcare, and trade. All people need incentive, pleasure, structure and respect to thrive. It is far better to give a hand up than to show apathy. We are a self-indulgent species. Everyone is entitled to pleasure along with having their basic needs met. It is not in our human nature to stand by idly and watch a neighbor thrive while we live a life of drudgery and sacrifice. Eventually one rises up in revolt. It is becoming apparent that a healthy global community benefits everyone. There is a proverb that says, "You can take no comfort from the hole in my end of the boat".

President Snow explains the history behind "The Hunger Games" in the televised propaganda before the reaping, "...War, terrible war. Widows, orphans, a motherless child. This was the uprising that rocked our land. Thirteen districts rebelled against the country that fed them, loved them, protected them. Brother turned on brother until nothing remained. And then came the peace, hard fought, sorely won. The people rose up from the ashes and a new era was born. But freedom has a cost and the traitors were defeated. We swore as a nation we would never know this treason again. And so it was decreed, that each year, the various districts of Panem would offer up in tribute, one young man and woman, to fight to the death in a pageant of honor, courage and sacrifice. The lone victor bathed in riches, would serve as a reminder of our generosity and our forgiveness. This is how we remember our past. This is how we safeguard our future."

When Primrose, Katniss' younger sister, "wins" the lottery as the female tribute from District 12, Katniss volunteers to take her place. The mail tribute is Peeta Mellark (played by Josh Hutcherson). Peeta is a shy young man who lacks confidence. Peeta and Katniss have not exactly been friends until now. They are taken to Capitol, the ruling district of Panem, for the Olympic event which begins with orientation and Opening Ceremonies. Seneca Crane (played by Wes Bentley) is the Head Gamemaker. After a training exercise, President Snow is irritated with Seneca, "An eleven," referring to Katniss' score, and Seneca says, "She earned it." President Snow clarifies, "She shot an arrow at your head," and Seneca corrects him, "Well, at an apple." But President Snow is not impressed, "Near your head. Sit down," and proceeds to explain to him how it is, "Seneca, why do you think we have a winner?"And Seneca says, "What do you mean," and President Snow amplifies, "I mean, why do we have a winner? I mean if we just wanted to intimidate the districts why not round up twenty-four at random, and execute them all at once? It would be a lot faster." Seneca doesn't have the answer and President Snow proceeds to tell him, "Hope," and Seneca is confused, "Hope?" President Snow explains, "Hope. It is the only thing stronger than fear. A little hope is effective. A lot of hope is dangerous. Spark is fine, as long as it's contained."

But Seneca Crane cannot contain hope especially when it's sparked by love. In a presentation interview, the colourful show host Caesar Flickerman (played by Stanley Tucci) asks Peeta, "So, Peeta, tell me. Is there a special girl back home," Peeta answers, "No. Not really." Caesar coaxes him, "No! I don't believe it for a second. Look at that face! A handsome man like you. Peeta, tell me," and Peeta confides, "Well, there uh...there is this one girl that I've had a crush on forever." Caesar wants the scoop, "Ah! " And Peeta adds, "But I don't think she actually recognized me until the reaping." Caesar prods him, "Well, I'll tell you what, Peeta. You go out there and you win this thing, and when you get home she'll have to go out with you. Right folks?" The audience cheers, and Peeta says, "Thanks. But I uh...I don't think winning's gonna help me at all," and Caesar asks, "And why not?" Peeta answers, "Because she came here with me," and Caesar gasps, "Well, that's bad luck," and Peeta says, "Yeah, it is." Caesar adds, "And I wish you all the best of luck," and Peeta says, "Thank you."

Peeta's sensitivity and charm, given his predicament, wins us over but Katniss is initially irritated by him. In a skirmish, he says to her, "I have no chance of winning! None! Alright? It's true. Everybody knows it. Do you know what my mother said? She said District 12 might finally have a winner. But she wasn't talking about me, she was talking about you." The night before the games they both have trouble sleeping and meet in the common room. Katniss says to Peeta, "I'm sorry I went after you," and Peeta tells her, "You know I meant that as a compliment." Katniss stares out the window and hears the crowd outside cheering for their tributes, and she says, "Listen to them," and Peeta says, "Yeah. I just hope they don't change me." Katniss asks, "How would they change you," and he answers, "I don't know. Turn me into something I'm not. I just don't wanna be another piece in their game, you know?" Katniss doesn't know, "You mean you won't kill anyone," and Peeta explains, "No. I'm sure I would, just like anybody else when the time came. But, you know, I just keep wishing I could think of a way to show them that they don't own me. You know. If I'm gonna die, I wanna still be me. Does that make any sense?" And Katniss says, "Yeah. I just can't afford to think like that. I have my sister," and Peeta empathizes, "Yeah, I know," and stares at her for a moment, "I guess I'll see you tomorrow." She smiles at him and says, "See you tomorrow."

Peeta's love bug creates media buzz and a winning strategy for "the star-crossed lovers from District 12". This gets them valuable sponsorship. After the 24 competitors are released into the war-zone amphitheatre, Peeta and Katniss bond romantically and in an underdog fight beat the odds and are the victors of The 74th Annual

Games. In art as in real life, no one wants to be owned or fettered.

7 | MOST OF US HAVE UNREALISTIC EXPECTATIONS OF WHAT IS POSSIBLE IN A DAY.

We drag our heavy to-do load around with us all the time. It's in our heads and it wears us out. It's a YouTube production. Press the reset button. A friend told me once that the "in-basket" is never empty. It's funny that it was a revelation to me. The thought had never crossed my mind before. Avoid measuring what isn't getting done and focus on what is being accomplished. Ask for help whenever possible.

If your life feels heavy, lighten up! Life is a series of steps. Take them one at a time. Not only is it easier, but it's the only way. Practice living in the present. Escape your mind trap by taking deep breaths that start in your tummy. Get into the routine of "dumping" what's in your head. If you write it down it reduces your stress level. Most of us love to-do lists and they are very handy. But those of us who live in our heads have a tendency to make long to-do lists.

If your to-do list for today has more than three or four things on it consider bumping some to the next day. What you have is not a to-do list for today but a wish list for the future. If you're dragging yourself from one place to another without a minute to spare you have too much going on. You've scheduled too many chores or appointments for yourself. Is it really a good thing to have your kids registered in two or three after-school activities every week? When your office hours extend routinely into the night, your lifestyle is not well balanced. You are taxing your body too much and sooner or later you'll burn out or suffer from sleep deprivation and eventually get sick.

The weight of responsibility usually falls disproportionately on those that accept the bigger load. Sometimes we are hesitant to say NO because we lack the courage. Other times we try too hard hoping to impress. I have learned that an occasional missed deadline is not the end of the world. Experience has shown me that there is usually more time. If you've ever attended an Emergency Room of a hospital, you've undoubtedly been made to wait. It may surprise you to learn that when you point out that a request is not reasonable people will reconsider and even respect you more for what you are doing. If you never speak up how is anyone to know what you're thinking? Some requests are preposterous. Most of us are only aware of how much we're doing and how long it takes us to do it. We always assume that it's a "nothing" task for someone else. That's being opportunistic!

When we plan our projects realistically we stand a better chance of achieving our goals. By letting others know what is possible and when it will be done we avoid bad surprises and disappointment. It is far better to be upfront with people than to have to postpone at the last hour or announce it won't be done. A short to-do list keeps us motivated to keep going. It's not a question of how much will be done but how much we expect to get done. We have to pace ourselves if we are to finish the race.

8 | GENEROSITY IS GIVING OF YOURSELF AND OF YOUR BEST.

Giving that which is not wanted or is to be discarded does not make one truly generous. When we get rid of our clutter it simplifies our lives. Someone else may get something out of it as a consequence. It's an easy and cheap way of getting rid of our unwanted items, some of which may be bulky. We feel good donating but sometimes the stuff we drop off is not any good. I've read that The Salvation Army spends millions of dollars annually on disposal fees and are becoming more selective with what they accept. While it may be nice to make these drop offs, it's not that generous. I believe that real generosity calls for a sacrifice. The act must have more heart than trade. For example, giving your sister your favorite skirt is hard; giving cash thins out your wallet; volunteering at a soup kitchen steals your time; babysitting your friend's children on your day off restricts your schedule. It does not have to get complicated. My mom would make a nice meal occasionally and take it to an elderly friend that was living alone down the street from us.

It is wonderful that so many organizations and individuals are philanthropic. Their dedication to improving the lives of billions of people around the world is admirable. They raise billions of dollars for goodwill and worthy causes: education, healthcare, human rights, enterprise, environment, arts, etc. Well-known philanthropists like Warren Buffet, Bill and Melinda Gates, and George Soros have given philanthropy a halo and they inspire others to join in. With their business acumen and connections they can do a lot of good. Bill Gates has been quoted on the web for saying, "Set your goal and then do charity."

There is no denying that these people are altruistic and generous with their time and their wallet. But why do most of them really do it? Because it makes good business sense. It earns them and their organizations goodwill, free advertising, acclaim, status, connections, and huge tax deductions. In April 2012, a plan by the Obama administration to cap tax relief on donations came under attack. There was a revolt by two-thirds of the ministers on both sides of the House, and many donors protested, so the plan was scrapped. Foreign Secretary William Hague said, "Some people have used charitable giving to reduce their tax bill to almost nothing." The Bible says, "For those to whom much is given, much is required." (Luke 12:48) The wealthy can do a lot more without asking for anything in return.

The most generous act is to listen patiently without argument or judgment. This is hard to do since we are primed to want to boast, defend, or attack. But when it happens it's amazing. Listening to someone unburden their soul is a true act of generosity. Much like blue skies can erase a blue mood, listening can soothe the spirit. An empathetic ear is medicine that can give relief to an aching body. Listening without revealing to another soul the personal content of what was said in confidence shows integrity and sincerity. That's true generosity.

Some of us enjoy hearing and spreading gossip a little bit too much and this has become a popular comic theme in sit-coms and movies. It's art imitating life all over again. In the 2010 film "Easy A", Olive Penderghast (played by Emma Stone) is a classy, clean-cut high-school student with too much of a generous spirit. To help some of the boys advance their causes, she agrees to go along with them spreading rumors about having sex with her. You can say that she donates her reputation and becomes a slut. It all starts in the girls' bathroom when Olive lies to Rhiannon (played by Aly Michalka), her nosy and domineering best friend, about a hot date, in order to get out of going camping with Rhiannon's hippie parents. They are overheard by Maryanne (played by Amanda Bynes) and a rumor about Olive losing her virginity that week end goes viral. The high school grapevine is abuzz with gossip.

Olive was a student under the radar till now. She likes the attention that the rumor mill is bestowing on her and doesn't mind being one up on Rhiannon for a change. Her little white lie is causing a stir. She is confident in whom she is and doesn't see the need to protest. Next, her gay friend Brandon (played by Dan Byrd) comes to see Olive. When Olive's mother answers the door, he asks, "Is there an Olive here," and she answers, "There's a whole jar of them in the fridge." But Brandon has a serious matter to discuss with Olive. He tells her he's being bullied and persecuted and begs her to help him out. She agrees to pretend making out with him at a party behind closed doors where everyone could hear. After that she gets approached by other nerds who need similar favors to advance their reputation as studs and are willing to pay her with worthless coupons and cash.

April has to contend with a circle of Jesus hypocrites, led by Maryanne, who have vowed celibacy and picket for Olive's expulsion. Maryanne says to April, "There's a higher power that will judge you for your indecency," and April glibly asks, "Tom Cruise?" Meanwhile, Maryanne defends her choice of a 22-year old boyfriend who is still going to her high school by saying, "If the good Lord had wanted Micah to graduate, he would have given him the right answers." Micah ends up contracting Chlamydia from the Guidance Counsellor, who happens to be the English Teacher's wife. Their antics infuriate Olive who has been brought up in a loving home with open-minded parents. She does nothing to dissuade anyone from thinking that she is not promiscuous or a prostitute. Rhiannon becomes so infuriated with Olive and what she's become that she joins the Jesus circle and calls Olive, "a dirty skank". At the height of her notoriety, Olive stitches a capital "A" on her laced-bodice tops, and parades through the school in scant, tight clothing. They are studying The Scarlet Letter and according to their popular English teacher Mr. Griffith (played by Thomas Haden Church), Olive is one of the few students who has actually read the book. When Mr. Griffith tries to find out why Olive is allowing the rumors to persist he says, "I don't know what your generation's fascination is with documenting your every thought... but I can assure you, they're not all diamonds." When the rumor mill becomes too much for Olive, she produces a webcast and reveals the whole truth to all. Those students in her high school awaiting more salacious details of sordid escapades were disappointed.

9 | ENTREPRENEURSHIP IS A WONDERFUL WAY TO CAPITALIZE ON YOUR SKILL SET.

If you have an idea for something that would solve a problem or satisfy a demand, and savings to fall back on, then you may want to start a business. Be realistic and conservative with your assumptions. While we all want to believe that our concept is a stroke of genius, the world may need time to come around to our idea. Running your own business has a long job description. You have to be willing to get down and dirty in the trenches. In the morning you may be dealing and weaving in a corporate boardroom while in the evening you're slugging away at your desk or in your shop. It may require that you work through the night so you can deliver the next day. When you're the sole employee there is no support or collaboration. When you're the boss, the weight of the business and the livelihood of those you employ, rests on your shoulders. You're responsible for everything. It gets lonely and stressful at the top.

If you think that it's freedom to do as you like, think again. Your clients and financiers are in charge. If you think it enables you to stay at home with your children, think again. Your children may be at home with you but you may not always be fully present to meet their needs. Many a times I had to motion to my child to be quiet so my client would not know that my attention was divided between daycare and their project.

In the 2010 film "Burlesque", Tess (played by Cher) is a retired dancer who owns a nightclub lounge in Los Angeles. Ali (played by

31

Christina Aguilera) is a small-town girl who's come to L.A. to chase her dream. When Jack (played by Cam Gigandet), the bartender, asks Ali why she left Iowa, she tells him "because there wasn't one person there I wanted to be like." Ali is charmed by the revue and tries to get Tess to give her a chance on stage but Tess has a full troupe and a full-hand of problems. Her situation is dire and it becomes clear when Tess' ex-husband and business partner comes to see her. He begs her to sell the club to a businessman who wants to tear the place down and build a development. It's the only way they won't lose everything. They can't pay the bills and will not be able to repay the mortgage loan which comes due at the end of the month. He tells her, "You won't talk to me before the show, after the show... It's like you're avoiding me," and Tess says, "I didn't divorce you to spend more time with you," and he tells her, "I may not be 'Mr. Tess' anymore, but I still own half this place."

Tess is one-hundred-and-fifty percent committed to the club. She choreographs the routines, is good with a glue-gun, and is mom and friend to her troupe. She not only has to worry about losing the place but has to deal with the troupe's problems which spill over into the club, like alcoholism and pregnancy. One of the girls has become a royal pain and when she comes in, Tess tells her, "You're probably not gonna believe this... but Sean and I were talking, and he said... I said, 'It's so sad that Nikki couldn't join us for the opening number...but it would be so great if she joined us for the next one," and Nikki answers, "Paws and claws. Took longer than I thought," and Tess says, so is finding a new job when I fire you," and Nikki answers, "Yeah, right."

Ali is determined to live out her dream. After being initially rejected by Tess, Ali picks up a tray and starts waitressing for Jack. When Tess sees Ali still there, she gets after Jack but then quickly gives in. A short time later, Ali gets robbed and Jack persuades her to stay at his place for a while. It's the beginning of something, but Jack's absentee girlfriend becomes jealous of Ali, so Jack pushes Ali to leave. When the girlfriend doesn't return as planned and Jack needs help paying the rent, he changes his mind but doesn't let on. Ali who is interested in Jack, knows the situation and repeats Jack's initial invitation for her to stay, back to him, "... but you're in a jam. And I'm the kind of guy... when a friend is in trouble, I help. It's just who I am."

Later, Ali tries to tell Tess that "she has the stuff" and has some ideas but Tess does not want to hear. She says, "People come here to watch the dancers dance... and to watch them lip-synch to the great singers." Ali has a soft approach, "I hear you. I get it. I'm just thinking of ways to make it better. I don't understand why we can't try...," and Tess tells her, "You don't understand because it's above your pay grade." Ali says, "I don't understand what that means. Hear me out. This is a good idea ...," and Tess tells her, "Ali, Ali, no– No. No. No." Eventually, with her big voice and big-stage presence Ali becomes the live attraction that raises the cash draw, but it's still not enough to save the place. Tess refuses to give up though and in a f-airy-tale ending Ali figures out a way of saving the place. The storyline is not so farfetched, although there usually isn't a fairytale ending in real life.

Most entrepreneurs are not rich and work long hours but there is satisfaction in creating something. Even if you don't really have control, you feel you do. It's better to try and fail then to not have tried at all. At least you know what was possible. In the 2003 film "Under the Tuscan Sun" Katherine says, "Regrets are a waste of time...they're just the past crippling you in the present."

10 | THE SOUND OF SILENCE CAN BE DEAFENING, ESPECIALLY WHEN YOU ARE NOT ALONE.

"If you say my name, there is no more. Who am I? (Silence)" It's a riddle that becomes a poignant game in the 1997 film "Life is Beautiful" (La Vita è Bella). The story is about an Italian Jew, Guido (played by Roberto Benigni who also wrote and directed the film) living in Arezzo, Tuscany, who has to hide his son Joshua (played by Giorgio Cantarini) from the Nazi guards in a concentration camp during the Holocaust. Guido convinces his little boy to keep absolutely quiet and still by playing a game. Upon their arrival, Guido pretends to translate the guard's instructions to the prisoners, "The game starts now. You have to score one thousand points. If you do that, you take home a tank with a big gun. Each day we will announce the scores from the loudspeaker. The one who has the fewest points will have to wear a sign that says 'Jackass' on his back. There are three ways to lose points. One, if you cry. Two, if you ask to see your mother. Three, if you're hungry and ask for a snack. Forget it!" Guido plays the game until the very end when in the chaos caused by the American advance, he hides his boy in a sweatbox to search for his wife Dora (played by the soft-spoken Marisa Paredes). She is not a Jew but went to the camp in protest and to be near her husband and child. Guido tells his son to not make a sound until everyone has left, as the final test for winning the tank. Guido is shot. When Joshua is reunited with his mother Dora, Joshua yells, "Mom. We won. We won. Hell yeah!!"

Silence cannot be had even when we can't hear a peep. The noise in our heads gets louder and louder as external sounds recede. That noise always trumps silence. Our mind is always crunching. Until we become aware of our thoughts they rule. Thoughts can race through the mind wildly causing us much distress. At every bump we jump to conclusions. It's the loud noise made by a broken motor running continuously and never stopping. The track scars our consciousness leading to more irrational thoughts and pretty soon our subconscious feels the injury. Our mood, our reason, and our feelings – all rely on a healthy mind. The funny thing is that the mind doesn't always get it right. Our thoughts are not always rational or true. The mind is easily fooled. This means that we can take control back. We can alter our thoughts and feelings as we wish.

There is nothing louder than the sound of silence when we're in a crowd. If there is someone else in the room and no one is speaking, then the space volume becomes deafening. Silence feels awkward when we are not alone. Whenever I hear a break in the conversation I want to jump in and obliterate silence. I used to believe that saying something would put the other person at ease. If there is silence between loved ones because of hurt feelings, then the silence is agonizing. When we are passive-aggressive we use silence as a warring tactic. The silent treatment is intended to take control away from the other party.

Silence is an interruption to give chance for an idea to surface. It's an opportunity waiting to happen. Now I try to give silence its' due time. When we allow our mind to wonder blissfully or give it a rest, we can drown out external sounds and feel tranquil. It's restorative and exhilarating all at the same time. The closer we can get to silence the more we discover ourselves. All we can do is set the noise level to the lowest setting. By tuning out external noise and listening acutely to our internal conversation, we can quell it. By immersing ourselves in prayer, meditation, contemplation, chanting, or simple repetitive actions, even for a few minutes, we can heighten our awareness and silence the world and ourselves.

Interrupt the chatter and suspend the urge to get carried away with your thoughts by taking deep breaths. A few minutes of deep breathing is like ten minutes of napping. Silence can be blissful if you learn to focus on what's in front of you. Gaze at the clouds for a prolonged instant. Marvel at the leaves blowing in the breeze. Enjoy a sunset. Talk to the moon when it's hovering close. Watch the waves as they roll back and forth from the shore. If you are alone then go for a walk or do some stretches. Any type of physical activity will relieve stress and interrupt the mind noise.

11 | WHEN WE REACT TO A SITUATION IN ANGER, IT ALWAYS MAKES IT WORSE.

Anger is the voice we use when we're hurting or when we're in pain. Insult or exasperation can cause us "to lose it" and release our pent-up fury. It's a temper-tantrum. We unleash a barrage of tactless words which cut like knives. Our anger is usually magnified by our body language. Our eyes bulge out, we blush, we stand erect, or we bang our fists. Our heart beats faster. Sometimes we get into someone's face. Without conscious breathing and stepping back, the intensity grows. The over-reaction overrides all judgment and lacks consideration or control. Some get physical and violate others. Heinous crimes are committed in anger, often between family members.

In the 2006 film "The Break up", Gary Grobowsky (played by Vince Vaughn) is a blokish Chicago bus-tour operator who meets Brook Meyers (played by Jennifer Aniston), an art gallery assistant, at a baseball game and charms her. They buy a condo and move in together but their relationship unravels when she gets saddled with all the responsibilities of hosting and cleaning, while he acts the part of a College fraternity roommate. Brook breaks up with Gary thinking that he will miss her and come to his senses. Instead their arguments spiral into a war of the sexes, as they try to sell their condo.

After one of Brooks pranks Gary loses it, "What kind of bullshit move was that," and Brooke answers, "I'm sorry, what? What happened?" Gary is angry, "Oh don't be coy with me. You sent that animal over here to attack me when I was hung over and weak." Brooke is coy, "Oh no. Look, all I know is The Tone Rangers they needed some place to rehearse so I very clearly told Richard stay in my room, which you explained to me was my space to do with what I want." Gary challenges her, "Is that how you want to play it? 'Cause I'll play it like that. I'll play it like Lionel Richie all night long lady. Oh yeah. I'll call some guys from my neck of the woods and we're not talking about, about a couple of queens who know a few grapples. We're talking about Polacks that don't have a goddamn future. That's right. We can make shit real uncomfortable around here and that's what we're going to do."

Brooke escalates it, "Please, come on. You know what, you're just embarrassed because Richard kicked your ass," and Gary says, "Richard did not kick my ass. What Richard did was attack me when I was half asleep," and Brooke taunts him, "Really, is that how you see it?" Now Gary's pride is hurt, "There's a real big gap between getting your ass kicked and having a dancing, singing sprite fool you with trickery and then strike your throat before you even know you're in a fight. But I wouldn't expect someone like you to understand that because all you do is make moves from up in your ivory tower."

Eventually the couple talks quietly. Gary finally gets her, "It's not about doing the things you love. It's about doing the things with the one you love." But it's too late. Brooke has given up on the relationship. Overcome with sadness, she says to Gary, "I just don't know how we got here. Our entire relationship ... I have gone above and beyond for you, for us. I've cooked, I've picked your shit up off the floor, I've laid your clothes out for you like you're a four year old. I support you. I supported your work. If we ever had dinner or anything I did the plans. I take care of everything. And I just don't feel like you appreciate any of it. I don't feel you appreciate me. All I want is to know, is for you to show me that you care." Gary sees how much she's hurting and says, "Why didn't you just say that to me," and she answers, "I tried. I've tried," and Gary tells her, "Never like that, you might have said some things that meant to imply that, but I'm not a mind reader..." It's too late. Brooke is done, "It wouldn't matter who you are. Just leave me alone ok? Right now, just shut my door." Gary tries to talk to her, "Listen," and Brooke says, "Alright Gary... just please, just leave the room Gary just ... I don't want to be near you right now, please just shut the door please."

Anger leaves resentment, hurt feelings, and regret. When we feel irritated by an action or a statement, we need to take a deep breath and count to ten before saying anything else. A delayed response rather than a reaction is usually more constructive. Postpone the conversation if the volume is raised. When we spiral into anger we lose the argument and at times the war.

Most parents have had to deal with children's tantrums. Usually we give them a time out and send them to a quiet place like their room. Sometimes my child would get so roiled up that I would have to hold him tight to prevent him from hurting himself. Thankfully he's grown out of that. When an adult has a temper tantrum we can't very well send them to their room. So what to do? Since we can only control what we do, it is best to get ourselves out of the line of fire. If there is any way that we can safely speak, then stating that we want time out is helpful.

We need to be disciplined in how we speak as well as what we say (our tone and our message). We have to be mindful not to over-react simply because we don't know what else to do. The saying "don't sweat the small stuff" can save us a lot of arguments. If we are frustrated because we're tired or bored then we have to be mindful not to take it out on someone else. If we're sick and tired of not getting any help and being saddled with all the chores we have to find a way to change the routine. The saying "you can catch more bees with honey than you can with vinegar" is apropos. If we've had a bad day we need to compose ourselves and chill out. Pause a moment or two and consider what you are about to say or do next. If emotions run high then it's best to say nothing and wait for a new day.

12 | CRISES ARE NOT FUN BUT THEY DO PRESENT OPPORTUNITIES...

Sometimes a crisis presents an opportunity to heal relationships and grow personally. A crisis can shake things up. Family feuds waste precious time and energy. Greed and arrogance are usually root causes. Pride and hurt keeps the feud going. The DNA strand between siblings and between parents and their children is vital. A broken connection has ramifications. The separation of loved ones is unnatural. Everyone loses. Anyone involved in a feud or a divorce knows how difficult and awkward it gets for everybody including those family members that are not feuding. Holidays are particularly painful. Celebrations become complicated. Children grow up without knowing their aunts or uncles or dads or moms.

Mending fences can be ever so simple yet so difficult to do. In the 2011 film "The Lost Valentine" Susan Allison (played by Jennifer Love Hewitt) is a successful TV journalist stuck in an unfulfilling relationship and distanced from her mother. She misses the closeness that Lucas (played by Sean Faris) has in his family. Susan and Lucas become romantically interested in one another but Susan who can't make up her mind about her boyfriend's marriage proposal, keeps Lucas at a distance. She is stressed about what to do but in her heart knows, "If you want to spend your life with someone, don't you want to feel excited," she says to her friend who is pressuring her to accept the proposal. Lucas is altogether different. He is a reputable physiotherapist who gave up being a baseball star to look after his grandmother and spend more time with his family. When Lucas tries to help Susan with her strained back, she says to him, "I know what you do. You mend people," In the end, Susan breaks up with her boyfriend and gets together with Lucas. She is inspired by Lucas' grandmother Caroline (played by Betty White) and their family bond and decides that it's time to mend fences with her own mother. When Lucas offers to accompany her on her trip to see her mother, she says, "Well that will be different," and Lucas says, "Sometimes different can be nice." Reconciliation is possible only when we decide to put aside the hurt and reach out. It's hard to do but always worth it. A crisis can help break through the resistance. Timing is everything. Lost time is unrecoverable.

13 | OUR CHILDREN ARE ENTRUSTED TO US FOR SUCH A SHORT WHILE.

Adults sometimes forget that children are persons that deserve respect too. Parents consider their children extensions of themselves – their heirs. We choose to interpret the Bible words "fruit of my loins" very literally. But children are not ours! They are treasures entrusted to us for only a little while for their safekeeping. Children are placed in our trust! They arrive in small packages, without gift wrapping. They are beautiful as they are. When my nurse presented my newborn baby to me, she said, "I checked him out and aside from a little peeling, he's perfect."

Babies are cuddly, innocent, and hungry. Dr. Phil likes to say that they are like sponges. We influence what they become. Perhaps that's the meaning of the Bible verse which tells us that the sins of the father can be visited down to three or four generations of future children. I don't believe for an instant that it's talking about retribution. No loving father would punish his children. Sadly, we can transfer our own dysfunctional habits to our children who then pass them on to their children.

The essence of humanity is the heart. It beats a drum – our heartbeat is time. It takes time to coach and inspire young minds. It takes discipline to control our frustrations. Our children need sweet love to grow up into loving human beings. It can be so simple if we are mindful. The word "okay?" enlists co-operation at any age. Play makes us fun to be around and teaches lessons without taxing the brain. Hugs make everyone feel better because we are embraced as we are. Inspiration begets commitment. Disappointment urges the spirit. Compliments prompt cooperation. Humor stifles argument. We can engage and motivate our children in so many ways. But we can't organize their lives into neat packages. Some lessons have to be learned in time. Our role is to prepare our children to fend for themselves in a world without us. Our joy is in watching them become accomplished in whatever they choose to do. We can watch them discover their lives!

14 | WIT AND HUMOR ARE SO UNDERRATED.

My mother's youngest brother is an old soul who's traveled a ways since his youth. As a young man he marched long distances across rough terrain, sometimes barefoot. He was drafted during World War II and then captured and taken to Kenya as a prisoner of war. After the war he returned home and then traveled north to France to find work and sent money regularly home to his widowed mother. After marriage, he immigrated to America to make a better life for his new family.

No matter how many times he's been uprooted, he thrives. He's always the life of the party – witty and amusing. He likes to dance and is quite comical to watch, especially now with his silky-white flock of hair. While he may act like a jester he's no fool. He's a self-made wealthy man. What you would notice first if you met him is that he's very loud. His voice pitch is high and startling. If you're unaccustomed to a larger-than-life personality, you will not appreciate him and that will be your loss.

In his early eighties he was shaken by a severe heart attack. We visited him in Intensive Care and he looked doomed. But he recovered and quickly returned to his regular daily tasks. He was 88 years old when his car was flattened by a truck on the highway. He was sandwiched in the wreck and they had to cut him out of the metal pile. Amazingly, he suffered only broken ribs. I guess when you're ravenous for life you don't let go too easily. How lucky for us.

15 | FEAR CAN BE DEBILITATING.

Most of us are ashamed to admit it but we are all afraid of something. Fear can follow us like a long shadow. When the fear is severe and irrational it is a phobia. An unmanageable fear for your life that grabs you repetitively is a phobia. It is a perceived threat that can handicap any lifestyle. I discovered I had several phobias as an adult. Standing on the edge of something or driving at high speed causes me great anxiety. I don't like climbing a ladder and I go to great lengths to avoid driving on the highway. When I started my business I had to visit a major corporate client, Nortel Inc., whose offices were readily accessible by highway. Upon leaving I was weary and not looking forward to the long drive back and happened to mention my challenge. My client told me in a very matter-of-fact way that the best way to conquer a fear is to face it. That's more easily said than done. When you're scared you can't see clearly, but when you're petrified you can't breathe.

On one of Oprah's televised road trips with her friend Gail, I learned that Oprah is uncomfortable driving on the highway. When Dr. Oz did a show on phobias he revealed that he too was afraid of heights. I admire them both enormously and learning this gave me solace. If they had phobias like me then I couldn't be that weird. Misery does like company but eventually, you get sick and tired of being afraid. It's personal! To conquer a phobia it is necessary to face it gradually if at all possible. A grand old lady I met one afternoon, when I took my child to a park in London, told me that after her husband died she was afraid to be home alone and would envisage herself cocooned in an egg. She cupped her hands like in prayer and told me, "You're safe in here." When I had no choice but to drive myself and my child on the highway to Toronto, I tried to envisage myself in that virtual egg while taking deep intentional breaths. I can report that it helped me miss a major accident which happened just ahead of me.

In the 2008 film "Nim's Island", Alexandra Rover (played by Jodie Foster) is the famous author of an adventure series of books. Alexandra is also an agoraphobic living a reclusive life in San Francisco. She's hardly ever ventured outside her apartment and has a neurotic relationship with the explorer Alex Rover, the main character in her books. Alexandra sends an email to Jack Rusoe (played by Gerard Butler), a renowned scientist living with his eleven-year-old daughter Nim (played by Abigail Breslin) on an island in a secret location in the South Pacific, wanting some information for her next book. It just so happens that Jack is off on a two-day expedition and Nim, is on the island all alone with her friends, Selkie the sea lion, Fred the lizard, and Galileo the pelican. Nim is very excited to receive the email from her favorite author, whose imaginary adventures rival Nim's real-life adventure on the island. She answers the email, "Dear Alex Rover... I'm sure Jack would love to help you with your newest adventure. He'll be back on Thursday. He's a great fan of yours. We both are. From Nim." Alexandra considers the reply, "Nim. Hmm, what an unusual name," then she writes, "Dear Nim, are you Jack's research associate? Jack wrote of a volcano where you live. Are you familiar with it? Sincerely, Alex Rover," Alexandra then continues conversing with her fictional hero Alex who tells her, "You've been writing chapter eight for three months now. So either sacrifice me to the damn volcano ... or let me find my escape already," and she interjects, "Hey! It's time to finish the book. Shh! I'm thinking." Alex answers, "Yeah. You're thinking. You're thinking. That's the problem. You've gotta get outta your head and into your body."

When Jack doesn't return from the sea, following a large monsoon rainstorm, Nim tells Alexandra about her dire situation. She emails, "Dear Alex, regarding your question 'Am I all right?' I will be when my dad gets back. But it's awfully good talking to a real live hero. Nim." Nim believes a story about how her oceanographer mother was swallowed up by a great blue whale when the Buccaneer's ship got too close and frightened the whale. Nim answers Alexandra, "Yes. I'm all alone. I'm 11, and my father's gone. He's lost at sea. And my leg is swollen and bleeding. And the Buccaneers are coming to take over the island. Nim." Alexandra realizes that Nim is a child and believes that she needs rescuing but Alexandra doesn't have the courage, "... I can't do this all by myself. I can't be the hero of my own story. I need you Alex Rover." She composes a reply to Nim, "I wish I could come but I'm a borderline agoraphobic," and Alex corrects her, "Borderline? Is that what you're callin' it? You're not actually gonna send that? Are you?" Alexandra continues with her mind dialogue, "I'm sorry. I wish I could come but I'm borderline agoraphobic. I haven't even left my apartment in 16 weeks," and Alex tells her, "What are you talking about? You're one of the great adventurers who ever lived. You're Alex Rover." Alexandra answers, "But I'm not that Alex Rover," and Alex tells Alexandra, "Yeah. You're definitely not."

Alexandra then tries calling 911 but it turns out they only perform rescues in the local geographic area. Then she calls the Department of the Interior for Fiji but they tell her, "There are 331 islands comprise Fiji. Ma'am." Nim tells Alexandra her exact location, "Our island is 20 degrees south, 162 degrees west ... in the south Asiatic Sea... Don't share my location with anyone else. My dad would be devastated if the world discovered our secret home. But I'm scared to be all alone. Nim." Alexandra has no choice but to set out to the island in the South Pacific and rescue Nim herself. She forces herself out of her apartment but it's obvious that just getting out the door is excruciatingly painful. Alex Rover, her imaginary hero urges her onward. Reaching the island would be a challenge for anybody never mind someone like Alexandra. Anything she could clutch to for relief is taken from her. She loses the dozen or so antiseptic cleansing bottles from her luggage at the airport. She's forced to remove her shoes and walk barefoot first at the airport and then on the boat. She has to change mode of transportation several times and neither the transit or the transport is ever easy. On the last stretch of the journey, Alexandra is dropped onto a cruise ship that has just left the island after Nim scared the tourists away from there. The ship's crew refuses to take Alexandra to shore and there's a storm. The tourists believe she's a lunatic. Alexandra has no choice but to jump into the ocean and swim to shore. She is saved by Nim and her sea lion Selkie. You can imagine the shock Nim has when she learns that Alexandra is Alex Rover. The contrast between the capable and independent young Nim and the crippled but motivated Alexandra is incredible.

16 | "ICE CREAM CHANGED MY FATE," SAID THE SEDUCTIVE KATHERINE...

I love the feeling of enchantment. It's that look that we see on children's faces as they discover each new day. I get it every time I look up at the sky through the tall trees of a wooded forest, or when I drive around a winding path and spy a country home nestled in a green valley, or when I stare at the horizon caressing the sparkling water of a lake or an ocean. Life is all about simple pleasures. In simplicity there is wonder.

The 2003 film "Under the Tuscan Sun" is a heart-warming drama about second chances in life. It's serendipity all the way! Frances (played by Diane Lane) travels to Italy, on a 10-day gay bus-tour ticket (a gift from her friends), after her marriage in San Francisco abruptly ends. On impulse – a moment of folly – she buys a villa in Tuscany. The villa is in total disrepair and becomes an unplanned project. With much frustration Frances sets out to repair it and in the process revitalizes her life. One of her teachers is the seductive and overly-dramatic Katherine (played by Lindsay Duncan) who tells her (and us) the secret to happiness: how to discover what the French say is "joie de vivre" and what Italians do very well – "vivere bene".

Katherine wraps up the whole storyline very simply in one scene. It's a chance evening encounter between Frances and Katherine in the piazza where everyone converges to party. The piazza is a meeting place. Frances is not accustomed to the frequent flirtatious passes made so casually by Italian men and Katherine has to translate,

"He's not asking when you last had sex. He's asking whether or not you're married." Frances politely answers the man, "Thank you. No, I'm not." And then there's another pass, "Everything all right darling?" Frances replies, "Oh terrific. I'm just eating." But Katherine corrects her, "He is." Frances blushes, "Oh, my God. I feel like such an idiot." Katherine reassures her, "Don't. Flirting is a ritual in Italy. Just enjoy it." Then she offers Frances her gelato, "Taste this. It's gorgeous." Frances takes a lick and wonders, "Mmm! How do you do it?" Katherine asks her, "Do what," and then proceeds to tell us the secret that everyone wants to know, "well hats make me happy. And ice cream. Ice cream changed my fate. It was because of ice cream that my beloved Fefe discovered me." Frances asks, "Fefe?" Katherine elaborates, "Il Maestro." But Frances still doesn't know, "Who?" And Katherine tells her, "Federico, darling." Frances guesses, "Fellini." But Katherine keeps talking, "He discovered me in the Piazza Novena with my parents eating an ice cream. I was gobbling it down, letting it run all over my chin because I was hungry. 'Do you like ice cream? He asked me.' I didn't know who he was. 'You are my imagination come to life,' he told me. He wasn't just a director. He gave great advice." Frances nudges her on, "I'm listening." Katherine elaborates, "Fefe said you have to live spherically in many directions. Never lose your childish enthusiasm and things will come your way."

In another scene, Katherine says to Frances, "How are you ever going to be happy if you keep wallowing? Listen, when I was a little girl I used to spend hours looking for ladybugs. Finally, I'd just give up and fall asleep in the grass. When I woke up, they were crawling all over me. So go work on your house and forget about it." But I digress... I couldn't resist. Let's get back to the topic of ice cream.

Ice cream is all about pleasure. It makes everything better at any age. (After all, real life inspires art and art imitates life.) If you have nothing else to do and want to relieve the boredom, you can go out to get an ice cream. If you're exhausted after hours of hard work, you can stop for an ice cream and lick it slowly while you recover. If you're out and about, and want to indulge in an inexpensive treat, you can buy an ice cream.

I can still remember the divine treat I had one evening as a small child "nel mio paese" in southern Italy. It cost a whole five Lira (about five cents) and it was to die for. It was the first "penguino" that I recall having – a chocolate-coated-creamy-gelato-on-a-stick. I walked about licking it slowly for as long as it lasted. If I close my eyes today I can still taste how delicious it was. It conjures up the joy I felt on a magical night of fireworks, music, and song. When I reached my teens, growing up in Toronto, I'd often share an ice cream with one of my five sisters. We didn't always have enough money for two. Sometimes we would walk to our destination in order to save the streetcar fare and buy the ice cream. It gave us so much pleasure. If we were out with our mother, she'd buy one for each of us but never one for herself. We would then grudgingly insist that she taste some of ours.

My child was treated to ice cream on most excursions. It was the least we could do to make up for all the hardship. Long and arduous trips to our "overnight place" were made bearable whenever we stopped half way at a place called Mayfield. It was really an undiscovered oasis with lots of trees and a river running through it. There was spring water to quench our thirst, beautiful white swans swimming in a large pond, and a water wheel for special effect. The place could not offer any more delight to the imagination. After a ride with his dad on a circus swing built for two, and a bathroom stop, my husband would walk him over to the trailer which was parked there all summer long. When they reached the ice cream window I could hear the question from afar, "What flavor?" and the answer was almost always the same. There is no doubt in my mind that ice cream is a heavenly concoction intended to keep us amused here in this earthly playground.

17 | ONE MAN'S TRASH IS ANOTHER MAN'S TREASURE.

People throw good stuff out for different reasons. They finish with it and no longer have a need for it. They don't have space for it. They no longer like it or value it. When we have excess, we value nothing. My mother grew up poor. She found a purpose for everything. In her day, recycling was not about having environmental consciousness or a popular trend. It was necessity. She was nine years old when her dad died and she was the oldest of four children. Their mother struggled to provide and the children had to help. They all had chores starting at a young age and were expected to do more before the age of ten than we entrust to our nineteen year-old teens. There was no safety net. There were no employers in her town. If you toiled, you ate, otherwise you went hungry. Everyone was an entrepreneur.

Nowadays, garbage collection is a lucrative industry. Everything is throw-away. It costs our cities a lot of money to handle our garbage. They collect the funds from us! Recycling is an expensive campaign. Our nations are all in debt. Most people live on credit. We buy storage containers but throw away packaging that could be used instead. It's a negative spiral of indulgence. When the pendulum swings too far one way, it will swing back the other way soon enough. We will learn that less is more.

18 | LAUNDRY IS AN ENDLESS CHORE.

I complain about the laundry more often than I do about the weather. There are always piles of clothes waiting to be washed. I sympathize with anyone that has a large family. My teen pulls clothes out of the chest drawers or closet, picks out what he wants, and throws the rest on the floor. When it gets picked up, it usually goes in the wash. Laundry reveals a lot about who we are. For example, laundry is an artful endeavor for my sister. She handles every item with care and does not want me anywhere near her laundry. Her clothes are important to her. She's a fashion aficionado. When I want to restore an item to its former glory, I ask her for a sisterly favor.

When I was growing up, the back yard was meant for the clothes line. The items on the clothes line revealed a lot about the occupants in the house. How many people live there? What gender? What do they do? How well off are they? I hate to think about what our clothes line said about my family. I was embarrassed by the rags that mom would often hang on our clothes line. But I must add that every item was spotless and bright. How did she do it?

Our laundry routine has changed dramatically over the years. When I was a child in Italy my mom would take the laundry down to the river and clean it in the running stream. The spot was very popular. It was a lively gathering place which came alive with laughter and song. The women would work heartily while singing loudly in chorus. Their songs filled the air and were carried happily by the rushing current of pristine water. I would watch my mom beat every item on a large rock separately and scrub it with a lump of hard soap that had been home-made from lard by her or a friend. Afterwards, the items were spread over large boulders to dry. Once or twice a year she would make a fire outdoors and boil a large tub of water to soak everything in. It was most important to boil the bed linen which covered our straw mattresses. It was an industrial operation.

By the sixties most homes had a washing machine. That invention made the woman's work considerably easier. It didn't faze her that she had to skillfully guide every item through the roller with precision in order to wring out the dirty water; rinse, roll, and repeat. I would giggle whenever a garment got caught in the roller which was often. It was fun to watch the roller run-a-muck. We've come a long way baby!

19 | FEAR CAUSES A "FIGHT-OR-FLIGHT" RESPONSE BUT SHOCK STOPS US IN OUR TRACKS.

We all know about our automatic "fight-or-flight" response mechanism which was originally intended to protect man from the proverbial sabre tooth tigers that once lurked in the woods and fields around us, threatening our very existence. This acute-stress response is now mostly ON because of the constant stress in our lives. Luckily we only need it occasionally to alert us to a dangerous situation, since we no longer have to hunt in the woods. But the mechanism is really a "fight-or-flight-or-freeze" response.

If we cannot see a way out of a frightening situation, we freeze. Shock can paralyze us. To feel safe we need predictability in our lives but the future is not predictable. We cannot control the actions of others. People do crazy things when they feel backed into a corner. They act out of fear, sometimes foolishly and with poor judgment. When the unthinkable happens, it is necessary to breathe deeply and compose ourselves quickly. Breathing deeply is like pressing the reset button. It enables us to think more clearly and mobilize our defenses. If we can run then that's the thing to do. If we can fight then that's what we should do.

In a crisis it is always necessary to summon help. Neighbors can come quickly to our rescue. Sometimes we must rely on strangers. In the 1997 film "Titanic", when the older Rose recounts the story to her grandchildren about her romantic encounter with Jack on the ill-fated Titanic, she said, "He saved me in every way that a person could be saved." No matter what we believe in, praying to an omnipotent force, can give us strength. We need to call out to our God, the Divine, the Universe, or even "mom" for help. It's so natural to cry out that we do it impulsively.

After an assault, our system needs time to internalize what just happened. The support of family and friends is essential to help us through tough times. We need to connect to them – they are our life line. We need tender loving care and a place to rest for a while. If we can immerse ourselves in inspirational verses or mystical beauty, we can get through the day. The sun always rises again.

Trauma puts us in a tightly-wound coil. With so much stored-up tension, any little thing can set us off. The 2012 film, "The Lucky One" is a portrayal of U.S. Marine Sergeant Logan Thibault (played by Zac Efron), who is traumatized by war. In the opening scenes, Logan is fighting on the front-lines. He returns to the States after serving his third tour of duty in Iraq. When he goes to stay with his sister's family he cannot cope with the normal routine. Logan is easily spooked by the children playing video games and jumping on him. He is wounded. "Why did I make it out when so many guys didn't? I feel like there's this debt that I have to pay. I don't know where I belong. I guess I should figure that out. I know there is no easy answers sis but maybe all I need is time," he tells his sister by webcam.

He goes searching for the person in the photo he found in the rubble in the war zone. On the back was written, "Keep safe. X". He believes that she was his "guardian angel" and wants to thank her for saving his life. (Just after he walked over to pick up the photo, an explosion when off which killed three men.) He finds her at Green Kennels in Louisiana but cannot find the words to express his feelings. His emotions are all coiled up. Beth (played by Taylor Schilling) thinks he's applying for a job there but after learning that he's a Marine and that he's just walked from Colorado, she tries to get rid of him. Beth's nana Ellie (played by Blythe Danner) says to Beth, "He looks harmless." She says to Logan, "My granddaughter thinks you might be crazy... You tell me why does a sharp, capable young man want a job cleaning cages?" And Logan tells her, "Because it seems like peaceful work. My last job wasn't."

Logan has a quiet manner about him and a seamless connection to his dog Zeus. He tells Beth that he loves walking as much as she loves running. It's cheap therapy. The serene country setting is a stark contrast to where he's been. The natural beauty and quiet rhythm are soothing to Logan's broken spirit. He is in a slow simmer. But the silence is deceiving. The extremity holds much tension and despair. The suppressed emotions are palpable. Beth lost her brother Drake about a year earlier. He was also a Marine. On the anniversary day, she cannot contain her grief and breaks down in the rose orchard. Logan runs out to restrain Beth. As he holds her, she pours out, "At first they wouldn't tell us anything. Just that friendly fire was a possibility... and the investigation ... is still ongoing. That's the worst part. Not knowing. I would give anything ... to know that he didn't die for nothing. We were inseparable. We did everything together. We even built that wall together. Well, Drake built the wall. I supervised... " Beth and Drake had lost their parents in a car accident when they were young.

When Ellie asks Logan to drive her to her choir practice, she chats with him, "How old are you dear," and Logan says, "Twenty-five." Ellie asks, "How many tours," and Logan answers in a matter of fact way, "Three." Ellie goes on, "My grandson never finished his second. Yah. You would have liked him. You two, you were cut of the same cloth. You know, you live long enough Logan, you lose enough people, you learn to appreciate the memories you have. You stop begrudging the ones you never got to make. Beth hasn't lived as long as I have. She isn't as bad as she seems." Logan says, "She doesn't seem so bad to me." Ellie smiles at him.

Logan and Beth become passionately involved. After love-making, Beth asks him, "Why did you come here," and he answers, "To find you." When the photo gets discovered by Beth's jealous ex-husband, Logan finally has to explain, "I just found it... I know I should have told you. I tried. I didn't know how." Beth says, "Try telling me now." And Logan relives the experience, "It was in the morning after a night raid. I just found it... in the middle of nowhere. I tried to find out who lost it. I never stopped trying but no one claimed it. Finding something like that in a war is like finding an angel in hell. So I kept it with me and I survived a lot of things. Things that I had no right to... I promised myself that if I made it out, I would find that girl and thank her for saving my life when others weren't so lucky. But I couldn't find the words. How do you explain something you can't even understand yourself?" Beth is angry, "Understand this. This was Drake's. It was meant to keep him alive," and Logan says, "I wish it had. I wish it had."

At the beginning of the film, Logan's voiceover tells us, "You know, the smallest thing can change a life. In the blink of an eye, something happens by chance, and when you least expected it, to set you on a course you never planned, into a future you never imagined. Where will it take you? That's the journey of our lives; our search for the light. But sometimes finding the light means you must pass through the deepest darkness. At least that's how it was for me." At the end of the film, he says, "Everyone has their own destiny. Not everyone makes the choice to follow it. I'm lucky I did."

20 | SOME EVENTS ARE MEANT TO CHANGE THE DIRECTIONAL FLOW OF OUR LIVES.

A storm can create a lot of debris on the beach but some of it will be swept away by the morning tide. No matter how intelligent or capable we are, we can get stuck in a lifestyle that is not working for us. Often we really want the change, which we know in our heads that we need, but cling stubbornly to the status quo indefinitely. Eventually we may even desperately long for the change but can't find the courage or the heart to make it happen. Feelings are void of logic!

Sometimes we are in denial and don't want to admit that there is a serious problem or a deficit in our lives. Other times we are naive and want to believe that things will change without us taking any action. The change we need may relate to an addiction or a relationship, a job, a house or anything else that affects our lives. In relationships, denial and naivety can fool us for a very long time into accepting consequences which are senseless, all in the name of love.

In the 2001 film "Ocean's Eleven", Danny (played by George Clooney) has just been released from prison and Tess (played by Julia Roberts) is there to pick him up. Danny says to Tess, "Hi," and Tess says, "We need to get Rusty a girl." Rusty (played by Brad Pit) is Danny's best friend and partner-in-crime. Rusty answers, "There's a woman's prison down the road." Danny looks at Tess' wedding ring and teases her, "You said you sold this," and Tess says, "I said that," and Danny says, "Liar," and Tess answers, "Thief." Later, in the hotel scene, Danny says to Tess, "You remember the day I went out for cigarettes and never came back. You must have noticed." Danny goes to sit down and Tess tells him, "I don't smoke. Don't sit!"

Rusty questions Danny's real motives for the job that is about to go down, "Tell me this is not about her or I'm walking? I'm walking off this job now," and Danny tries to deny, "Who?" Rusty goes on, "Tess. Terry Benedict. Tell me this is not about screwing the guy who is screwing your wife." Danny corrects him, "Ex-wife," and Rusty doesn't let him off, "Tell me." Danny clears it up for Rusty, "It's not about that … It's not entirely about that. [Rusty is furious with him.] Russ, do you remember what we said back when we first got into this business? We said we were gonna play the game…," and Rusty interjects, "like we had nothing to lose." Danny goes on explaining, "Well, I lost something. I lost someone… that's why I'm here." But Rusty who is not blinded by love says, "Okay, here's the problem. We're stealing two things and when push comes to shove, and you can't have both, which are you gonna choose? And remember, Tess does not split eleven ways!"

In a relationship, we usually expect our partners to change. We assign blame to the other party. We become co-dependent. Danny says to Tess, "Now they tell me I paid my debt to society. And Tess tells him, "Funny, I never got my check." No matter what, a round peg does not fit a square hole. Our parents stayed together no matter what. They believed that their children were better off with both parents living under the same roof. Until recently, a woman without a man walked with shame, like a scarlet. Thankfully our views have changed somewhat in this regard but there is still a lot of stigma associated with family breakup. Often we take too long to move on.

A storm can blow things apart. It forces us to deal with the situation. When our hand is forced, as is the case when we lose our job or we lose our partner – we have a chance to change our predicament and possibly make things better. The unexpected event releases us from our cage and frees us to make new plans. The recent economic downturn, for example, has created challenges but also opportunities for people to take control of their debt load or start a business. A new beginning is a chance at a better life.

21 | MY HEART IS YOUR HARBOR AND MY ARMS YOUR SHELTER.

We are all nomads wandering on this earth of ours, vulnerable to the natural elements. When I was a child, gypsies would sometimes come through our town. They were a colorful and mysterious bunch travelling in groups like herds. As they roamed from one place to another, the wind would stir. They were not welcome anywhere. I never saw them. I only heard of them and was convinced they were invisible. The news of their arrival would spread quickly with old fashioned instant-messaging. Gypsies had a reputation for stealing so no one really wanted to give them shelter. Once I heard my mom saying that they were staying in our barn. I was seriously afraid and intrigued at the same time. Everyone feared them. They were thought to possess magic powers, capable of casting voodoo spells. I overheard town folks saying that if you mistreated them or refused them they would curse you. I believed it to be true and hoped I would never cross their paths.

Some of us wander aimlessly alone and lost even when we have lodging. In the 2007 film "August Rush" Louis (played by Jonathan Rhys Meyers) and Lyla (played by Keri Russell) are two strangers who meet on a rooftop one evening. They are both popular musicians trying to get away from the crowds. Until that fated night, they were two souls travelling alone on separate parallel paths. A sweet melody flirts with the wind and fills the October air. On the New York City street below, there's a fellow strutting past the city square arches with a guitar, playing a soulful serenade on his mouth organ. Louis startles Lyla from a ledge up high, "It's a great sound. Isn't it," and she looks up and says, "What are you doing," and he answers, "Listening. What are you doing," and she is embarrassed, "I just came up to ... um... to...", and he says what she wouldn't say, "get away?" They smile at one another empathetically. Louis invites Lyla to join him on the ledge, "Have a seat. Com'on. Be brave. Front row center."

Lyla climbs the ladder and sits next to him. She's embarrassed by his stare. He gazes at her and then looks up at the moon, contemplating them both. He asks, "Can you hear that," and she answers, "what is that?" She's curious to know the name of the tune which escapes her as a world-class artist. But Louis hears a lot more in the music, "It's a wish." His gaze turns up and he fixes on the glaring moon. She looks at him with intrigue, smiles, and looks up, "What does that sound like," and he answers with a song, "Well, it's a marvelous night for a moon dance, with the stars up above in your eyes. A fantabulous night to make romance, 'neath the cover of October skies."

Then in an earnest voice he tells her, "When I was a young fellow...I used to talk to the moon." Lyla thinks he's pulling her leg, "Are you making that up?" Louis continues as if he's thinking out loud, "God, I haven't done that in a long while." Lyla picks up on his sincerity, "Does it ever talk back," she asks him. "Well, it used to. Now I just find myself on a roof talking to myself...like a loon, just out here on my own." Lyla talks to that little boy inside him and tells him, "Well, I'm here," and Louis takes her hand and says, "Yes, you are. I'm Louis," and she says, "Lyla." Louis asks her, "So, what's your story Lyla?" Lyla ponders for a long minute and then answers, "I don't know. I'm just ... I'm just me...," and Louis stares hard and deep, looking into her soul, and she asks, "What are you looking at?" Louis answers, "You."

Louis and Lyla kiss sweetly and spend the night together on that rooftop. The next morning they're woken abruptly by Louis' brother and the other two band members. They all have planes to catch leaving New York City that morning. Lyla rushes to put her sandals on, "Oh my God... I have to leave." But Louis doesn't want her escaping, "Let me walk you home," and Lyla says, "No. My dad's waiting at the Sherry.... I – I've never done this before." Louis tries to hold on to her, "Hey. Hey. Meet me here at 10:00 by the arch... Say yes." He gets some help from his brother, "Put him out of his misery. Say yes," and Louis pleads, "say yes...," and his brother pleads, "say it." Lyla is anxious and looks back at Louis warmly as she disappears into the staircase. Louis tells her, "I'll take it as yes." When she doesn't show up at the arch, he rushes to the Sherry and sees her on the sidewalk outside the hotel, frazzled. He calls out to her and we can see that she's torn. Lyla's father directs her to get into the limo NOW and Louis watches her drive away. He is deflated and says to his brother, "What am I gonna do now?" A couple of months later he quits on life, "What's the point in singing, Marshall? She's not gonna hear me. I'm leaving the band. I'm sorry Marshall." When Louis faces his brother again years later he begs him, "Hit me... Hit me... I'm suffocating here." Lyla cannot forget Louis either; she carries his baby. After an accident supposedly causes her to lose the baby she also quits on life. For the next eleven years they both wander aimlessly and lost in different cities until one day their paths cross again and everything is made right.

We are all gypsies really. We all need somebody – a soul mate, a friend, a host. Most people don't like to put themselves out too much, not even for family. House guests may be fun for a day or so but pretty soon it feels like they have overstayed their welcome. We like our privacy and taking someone in even if it's only for a while feels intrusive. We don't so much mind helping someone who is stranded temporarily, because of a storm for example, but we would not feel comfortable taking in a homeless individual. Kindness is an act of selflessness. It takes so little to reach out and help someone and every act of kindness makes the world a better place. Our good intentions must be followed with good deeds. One good deed deserves another and that's paying it forward. Our circumstances can change in an instant. Our children watch what we do and emulate. What they live as children, they become as adults.

22 | "IF ONE DAY IS CRUMMY, THE NEXT HAS TO BE BETTER." IS THAT RIGHT?

I heard Meredith Vieira say this was so in an Anderson Cooper interview and she would know. Her husband Richard Cohen has battled multiple sclerosis for over 40 years. She also said that when one person in the family has a disease, the whole family gets it. The family is in it together. Her advice is to look for the bright side every day and always ask for help when you need it.

Coping with mental illness is hard because the very tool needed to effect change is compromised. The brain is complex and not well understood, and while research is advancing our knowledge, we are still prisoners of the mind. Getting help for someone suffering from a mental illness is a challenge. If you don't feel sick, can't see the disease, and there is a stigma associated with having the disease, why would you want to embrace it? Our mind plays tricks on us with memory, perception, desire, emotion, and mood. If, for example, we lose our memories, we lose ourselves. If we visualize a beautiful vista, we can improve our mood. It doesn't even have to be real. If we listen to soothing music, we lessen our pain. The brain has a duality which is hard to grasp. While it may be hardwired to the rest of us, it is elastic with a virtual capacity. It is known now that the brain can regenerate and if necessary can transfer a function to a different part of itself – real metamorphosis.

We have so much untapped potential in our brain that it's mind-boggling. The 2007 film "August Rush" is about a child raised in a boys' home in New York unbeknownst to the mother who was told her son died at birth. August, played by Freddie Highmore, grew up believing that the music he hears in his head is a call from his parents and at the age of 11 sets out to find them. "I like to imagine that what I hear came from my mother and father. Maybe the notes I hear are the same ones they heard the night they met," he tells us. While on the run in New York City, he is discovered by a homeless "crazy" pimp, played by Robin Williams, who recognizes the exceptional gift the boy possesses. In the fairytale, circumstances change and the boy ends up studying at The Juilliard School of Music. Here, the child prodigy is truly appreciated and is invited to conduct the New York Philharmonic Orchestra on the great lawn of Central Park. His mother and father hear his rhapsody and rush to him. In real life it may be different, but we've all heard of people with exceptional talents that cannot be explained. There is magic and malice in the mind. It's the source of our smiles and our sorrows.

23 | WE ALL ASPIRE TO BEING PATIENT AND LOVING WITH OUR CHILDREN, BUT THEY DO TRY OUR PATIENCE.

There are times when we are so stressed that we lose it. On those days our children are generous with us and are ready to forgive us. They can put up with an occasional outburst as long as we've infused them with love ahead of time. Tough love may be needed to correct bad behavior but sweet love can prevent it. We must treat our children with the same respect that we expect ourselves. When we stumble, it is important to say sorry. If we had a dysfunctional upbringing, then we need to learn how to parent. It is far better to persuade than to punish. Criticism is not helpful in shaping a personality, it corrodes it.

Thankfully, most of us don't believe that "spare the rod and spoil the child" is the way to discipline in a civil society. Physical punishment is abhorred in all situations and yet some still believe it is appropriate with our children. It may be easier or more expedient but it is wrong. When we spank or beat a child it's because we are unwilling or incapable of doing better. It's a reflection of us. Those of us who grew up when the strap or the stick was used in the classroom can speak to whether or not that did anything to help with learning. Corporal punishment does instill fear in the victim but fear is a basic primal emotion we share with animals. Fear is debilitating and can only affect primal responses. The imagination is a more sophisticated area of the brain; it's more easily accessible than memory. The imagination is an elastic muscle which brings something into existence. If we can engage creatively we can make meaningful change.

Often the injury we cause our children does not leave scars on the surface but creates deep emotional wounds which take years to heal. In the 2012 film, "A Thousand Words", Jack (played by Eddie Murphie) visits his mother (played by Ruby Dee) and finally listens to what she's been trying to tell him for a while. When he approaches, she believes Jack is her dead husband Raymond, "Raymond, you finally came. Sit. Tell me what you have been doing. It's my birthday. Do you want some birthday cake? What? You can't talk? Your throat... I have so much to tell you. It's so nice here... I've got all my things here. But sometimes I get lonely. Raymond, I get so ... but then I can always count on Jack. Jack always comes. He brings me flowers. He helps me and when we go for walks all the ladies are so jealous because he's so handsome. Aha ha ha! I'm just so proud of him, Raymond. See, you missed Jack growing into the greatest man. He's amazing. He can do anything. Jack is my only reason to live. But... he's so angry. Mad at you. Mad at himself. I think he believes you left because of him. He was just a kid but he carries that anger every day. I wish he would let it go. He would be much happier if he would let it all go. Raymond, you need to tell Jack how much you love him. We're family. Life is not worth living without family. Right? Right? ... Isn't someone going to sing to me? I like cake. Don't you Jack?" And Jack kisses his mom on the forehead and says, "Bye ma. I love you."

Jack then visits his father's tomb in the cemetery and hears the ghost of his younger self saying, "I missed you. I saw you a few times... and then you left... and then it was a long time... and then you died. I guess you never know if the last time you see someone is the last time you're going to see someone." The older Jack finds his voice and says to the boy, "I wish there was a way I could make it up to you." And the younger self says, "There is. Chase me. Com' on." And Jack uses up his last words, "I forgive you," and is healed.

What I remember most fondly about my dad is his playfulness. Hugs and humor are great motivators. My son is strong willed and tests my patience frequently. I resist getting into a power struggle with him as much as possible. When he was little I would do this by changing the topic or by injecting love or humor into the situation before he spiraled into a tantrum. Avoiding tantrums requires good sense and perfect timing.

There is pleasure to be gotten from sweet discipline. Sometimes all you have is your wit to effect change. A long drive is stressful, especially on children, and bound to test everyone's patience. "Tiger, I'm going to send you back if you don't behave," I warned him. "You can't do that!" he countered. "Yes I can. I'm calling God on the telephone to ask him to expect a delivery," I told him. "God doesn't answer the telephone," he argued. "Then I'll email him. He's on the Web," I said, but he wasn't to be outsmarted, "Ha, ha. You can't do that mom." I stretched it a bit longer, "There must be a way. I won't stop 'till I reach him." And we laughed together out loud. We had forgotten what started it.

24 | OUR LIVES CAN CHANGE ON A DIME.

Sometimes the event is unexpected. Other times we just weren't paying attention to the signs which were posted along the way. I remember Oprah saying once that the universe gives us lots of warnings starting with a gentle tap on our shoulder. When we're not listening, the tap gets louder and louder and if we're still not paying attention, we get thumped on the head. Our intuition is a fine-tuned antenna. When a little voice in our head says, "something is wrong", it's usually best that we heed the warning.

Often, we are too stubborn or have chosen to bury our heads in the sand. I am not referring to those of us who worry all the time about everything. That's just a habit which needs a reality check. When you are not feeling like your usual self or when in a relationship you can't speak your mind, not even softly, then there is a problem that you need to address. There may be a health issue or there may be abuse. Don't allow yourself to be caught by surprise. It is far better to change your circumstances than to become hostage to them. My mom used to say that one should always have an emergency stash to fall back on. My dad would never go anywhere without money in his pocket. Make a plan for how to cope with an emergency, whether it is a fire escape route in your home or a shelter to run to. Prepare for unforeseeable events because they don't only happen to someone else. Sometimes they happen to us.

Focus on your goal. Rise above your predicament and look at the bigger picture. "Don't bite off your nose to spite your face," means don't cause yourself grief by retaliating or over-reacting. Blame does not persuade anyone or improve anything. Anger will not cure an injury only aggravate it. Guilt and regret are downward spirals. Shame contaminates the spirit. Secrets embolden the perpetrator and trap the victim. It takes too much energy to pretend and hide the truth. Besides, everyone is focused on their own life. Your situation is usually a side-show. If we feel trapped in our circumstances or anticipate an undesirable event, we need to prepare and take charge. We must be pro-active. We must act responsibly. We may need help. Often we don't ask because we don't want to burden others but that's what family and friends are for. Always look for the bright side and you'll find it. It's amazing what we can accomplish when we get on with it. Eventually you will arrive at forgiveness and acceptance. The sun rises in the morning. In a crisis we need support not sympathy.

In the 2000 film "Cast Away", Chuck Noland (played by Tom Hanks) is a productivity analyst with FedEx who gets stranded on an uninhabitable island after his plane crashes in the South Pacific. A photo of his girlfriend Kelly Frears (played by Helen Hunt) and a basketball he names "Wilson" help him survive for four long years. Finally, he rigs up a life-raft and returns home only to find that Kelly is married with a child. His friend Stan (played by Nick Searcy) explains to Chuck what happened after his crash, "Chuck, Kelly had to let you go. You know? She thought you were dead. We buried you. We had a funeral, a coffin, a gravestone, the whole thing." Chuck asks, "You had a coffin? Well what was in it," and Stan says, "Well, everybody put something in. Eh... just a cell phone, a beeper, some pictures. I put in some Elvis CD's." Chuck catches on, "So you had my funeral and then you had Mary's funeral. Stan, I'm so sorry I wasn't around when Mary died. I should have been there for you. But I wasn't. I'm so sorry."

Towards the end of the film, Chuck drops in on Kelly. It's late at night and her husband and child must be upstairs sleeping. Chuck and Kelly are chatting in her kitchen and she explains on the map the logistics of the crash and the search. Chuck gets around to the gritty stuff, "I never should've gotten on that plane. I never should've gotten out of the car," and Kelly asks him, "So what now?" Chuck answers, "I don't know. I really don't know." Chuck gets into his car which Kelly had kept and she says to him, "You said you'd be right back," and Chuck tells her, "I'm so sorry," and Kelly leans through the car window and kisses him, "Me too." As he drives off, she runs towards him in the rain and at the end of her driveway he gets out and she jumps into his arms and they kiss, "I always knew you were alive, I knew it. But everybody said that I had to stop saying that ... that I had to let you go. I love you. You're the love of my life." She gets into the car with Chuck. He goes to start the car and she says, "Chuck," and he looks at her knowingly, "You have to go home?" Kelly nods her head.

At Stan's home, Chuck says, "We both had done the math. Kelly added it all up, knew that I had...had lost her. 'Cause I was never gonna get off that island. I was gonna die there, totally alone. I mean I was gonna get sick, or get injured or something. The only choice I had, the only thing I could control was when, and how, and where that was gonna happen. So... I made a rope and I went up to the summit, to hang myself. I had to test it, you know? Of course. You know me. And the weight of the log snapped the limb of the tree, so I... I... I couldn't even kill myself the way I wanted to. I had power over nothing. That's when this feeling came over me like a warm blanket. I knew, somehow, that I had to stay alive. Somehow, I had to keep breathing. Even though there was no reason to hope. And all my logic was proven all wrong because the tide came in and gave me a sail. And now, here I am. I'm back in Memphis, talking to you. I have ice in my glass. And I've lost her all over again. I'm so sad that I don't have Kelly. But I'm so grateful that she was with me on that island. And I know what I have to do now. I gotta keep breathing, because tomorrow the sun will rise. Who knows what the tide could bring."

25 | I AM A PROCRASTINATOR.

It's not that I am lazy but I get overwhelmed and even intimidated at times. The load seems so heavy and the tasks too hard. I don't understand how it is that when I had much more on my plate I managed to get it all done. It makes me think that my affliction has nothing to do with the load. A deadline always gets me moving but I cut it real close and end up burning the midnight oil.

It doesn't help that I am also a perfectionist. You won't be surprised to hear that I've suffered "burn-out" more than once. I used to take pride in being a perfectionist but I've learned that it has more to do with arrogance than standards. Nothing is ever good enough. I want it better. It stands to reason that I can't settle or decide on one thing. Perhaps it's a fear of failure. As I see it, the more options the better. If I don't exclude anything then I'm accepting everything. That's bound to lead to confusion and mediocrity, and an exacerbated need to procrastinate. Realistically we can't do it all and we can't have it all. There is risk in every choice we make. Perfection is a perception – not a reality.

When our expectations are unrealistic or blurred we get discouraged. The problem is that we don't stop to consider what "all" means. All is so abstract and confounding and because it's all too much to contend with, we may end up with "nothing". If we can figure out what we want or what we want to achieve, we have a better chance of getting there. We have to break down "all" into "certain things".

Once I start a task I am driven to complete it so the trick is to do something… anything which breaks through the resistance. That's where post-it notes and to-do lists help. If you can get it out of your head, it's a first step. I keep notepads nearby ready to scribble thoughts down. If you can coax yourself into doing only 10 minutes right then and there, it's a second step. Later is not an option for a procrastinator. One of my favorite lines from the 2011 film "The Lost Valentine" is when the older Caroline (played by Betty White) is talking about living life in the moment because later may not come, and says 'I don't believe in (the) meantime. Life happens all the time," and later she adds, "These days you can't put things off." Sometimes I leave a file where I can't miss seeing it. If it's an eyesore it will get your attention. If the task cannot be completed in one day, then make a schedule and stick to the same routine.

Staying disciplined is hard when we're not accountable to anyone or when we don't see progress. Introduce some accountability by telling a friend casually about your commitment. It may prompt you to act before they ask about it. If you can't bear the nagging or the embarrassment, then remind yourself with email or text messages or planner. Failure can set us back so be sure to schedule a reasonable amount of time for each task in your day. Often we are too ambitious and we forget to allow for regular activity like every-day interruptions, meals, and checking the mail. A challenge or a reward can motivate us to make good progress. Inch by inch, it's a cinch.

In the 2011 film "One Day", Emma, played by Anne Hathaway, is discouraged about getting nowhere with her writing. (It takes her over 10 years to write her novel.) She telephones her best friend and secret love Dexter, played by Jim Sturgess, and pours out her frustrations. "London swallowed me up. I thought I'd make a difference but no one knows I'm here," she says to Dexter, the sensitive but spoiled and forever-late-to-everything playboy who is vacationing in Paris. "Listen. Listen. Nothing truly good was ever easy," he tells her. "Who said that," she asks. "Why you did," he answers. "Did I? That's annoying," she adds.

26 | HOME-MADE PIZZA TASTES DIFFERENT FROM STORE-BOUGHT PIZZA.

Fresh ingredients and herbs add so much flavor to pizza. Home-made pizza has none of the unhealthy preservatives such as extra salt and nitrates. I used to make pizza often and when I did, I felt like a home-maker. It wasn't hard to do – kneed the doe, wait for it to rise, cover with favorite toppings, and bake it. I would change the toppings on each half to accommodate individual likes and dislikes. My husband could not eat cheese so I would exclude it and top that section with extra of other ingredients. I haven't made pizza for many years now which is indicative for me of a listless life. It's much easier to just buy it. It bothers me that I never made my home-made pizza for my son. My sister makes great pizza but my son won't give it a chance. He's concluded that the store-bought version is better. Could it be because that's what he's always eaten? He likes rich foods – salty, fatty, soggy, and sweet that is. I go on at nauseam about making better choices hoping that some of what I say sticks. He's convinced that he doesn't need to worry about health issues yet, if ever. I'm told that his views are typical of his age group.

I saw first-hand how bad choices can cause severe injury. Our actions may seem harmless or innocuous at first but repetition has consequences. My dad would not quit his life-long habits of smoking and drinking, not even after his stomach ulcers started bleeding. By the time he had a stroke and was unable to do either it was too late. The damage was already done. My mom suffered from emphysema even though she never smoked a day in her life and while this disease led to heart failure, her stomach was a constant irritant which made her final years intolerable. Her stomach problems were caused by poor diet which started when she was young and deprived. Experience tells me that our taste buds limit us to the same foods – good or bad. As we get older they become desensitized and we need more spice to get similar sensation. My mom craved bread, fat, and salt which were all bad for her. Our addictions and bad habits can cripple us and cause us much grief. Today, most of us are not deprived, yet we make poor choices nonetheless. So much of what we consume comes out of a store box. We opt for quick meals with minimal preparation and no clean-up. Meals are over with little fanfare. Our drive-through order gets us poor nutrition and minimal gratification.

Since we do precious little to infuse vigor into our lifestyles, we are left starved for life. When I was growing up our kitchen was a bustling place. We had a large house but all the activity was concentrated in the kitchen. Visitors were always ushered directly into the kitchen and within minutes there was a buffet on the table. Every meal was had at the table with everyone present, and it was not unusual for friends and relatives to drop in and join us. There was always enough food for company. It's unhealthy to eat alone. I remember that time very fondly.

27 | BEING SINGLE AND INDEPENDENT IS HARD TO DO.

Until recently, the only way that one could escape marriage without being ridiculed or shunned from the social scene was to become a monk or a nun. A person who is single has to put up with stigma and adapt to a society which is designed optimally for couples. This is the way it's been for centuries and this is pretty much how it still is today. Marriage is an ancient institution and one of three yokes on society; the other two are religion and poverty. The union between a man and a woman is not only necessary for legitimized procreation but for economic prosperity. While we want to believe that love and passion are the emotions that bring two people together naturally, this is only true some of the time. The betrothal of two people at a young age was and still is in some cultures, a reason to rejoice. The arrangement is usually made through a matchmaker and there is honor, satisfaction, and property involved in the transaction. Matchmaking used to be a deal in which the woman was bought or sold based on family status. Other property was exchanged as an equalizer. Parents dreaded the idea that their daughter would get to an age in the higher teens, let's say the ripe old age of 19, without a suitor. In contrast, the man's eligibility increased as he matured because with years he accumulated wealth. Since only men were allowed to own property and women were considered property, men stood to gain under all circumstances. It's not a stretch to say that when a boy was born parents felt lucky!

In the 2003 film "Mona Lisa Smile", Katherine Ann Watson (played by Julia Roberts) is a modern woman in the 50s who accepts a position teaching Art History at the prestigious Welesley College for young ladies. She wants her Welesley girls to progress and break free of societal barriers by thinking for themselves. But Katherine learns early on that her liberal ideas are not at all popular. When one of her students, Betty Warren (played by Kirsten Dunst) publishes an article in the College paper which ridicules her and attacks the values she espouses, Katherine has had enough. The class has no idea of the fury they have unleashed in Katherine. She begins a slide-show lecture, "Contemporary Art." The timid Connie Baker (played by Ginnifer Goodwin) interjects, "Now that's just an advertisement." Katherine slams her, "Quiet. Today you just listen. What will the future scholars see when they study us? A portrait of woman today? There you are ladies. The perfect likeness of a Welesley graduate. Magna Cum Laude doing exactly what she was trained to do. Slide. A Rhodes scholar. I wonder if she recites Chaucer while she presses her husband's shirts. Slide. Hey, now you physics majors can calculate the mass and volume of every meat loaf you ever make. Slide. A girdle to set you free! What does that mean? ... What does that mean? ... What does it mean? I give up. You win. The smartest women in the country... I didn't realize that by demanding excellence I would be challenging... what did it say?" She walks over to a student's desk and picks up a newspaper and then continues, "What did it say? Um... the roles you were born to fill." She looks up at Betty, "Is that right? The roles you were born to fill? ... It's, uh, it's my mistake." She drops the paper in disgust and walks out of the classroom, "Class dismissed." Later she says to her colleague and romantic partner Bill Dunbar (played by Dominic West), "I thought that I was headed to a place that would turn out tomorrow's leaders, not their wives."

In my lifetime, which relatively speaking is not that long, I've witnessed matchmaking, gender preference, and status bias. I lived the storyline of "Mona Lisa Smile". When I was a teen, marriage was the popular career choice for most girls. The romantic dream held such an allure that it was hard to resist. If you asked a girl what she was going to do in life, she would say, "I'm getting married." Marriage was an occupation which snarled both girls and boys for life except that boys had more liberties and were matured by age, whereas girls were ruled and diminished by age. Like everyone else, I dreamed of falling in love but it was not an obsession. The fairytale simmered at the back of my mind. My first wish was to go to university and become a doctor but I didn't talk about it in case it stirred up a protest which could be fuelled by gossip. High school was seen as a playground where boys talked to girls directly and that was not allowed. Risky behavior like that could lead to "trouble". Strict rules gave way to gossip and as a result, my older sister, who was the only sibling to attend high school ahead of me, quit school in grade 10. I would be the first in my family to attend university, and a girl at that. Yet, no one tried to dissuade me from what I wanted to do. My parents seemed pleased and proud, even if they never said so.

After graduating from university I embarked on a career. It quickly dawned on me that most of my friends were already married and with children. Was there something wrong with me? I prayed for my prince charming to show up soon and save me from a fate of becoming an old spinster. As it happened he showed up just in time. It was love at first sight. He was a heartthrob in his tight blue jeans and checked shirt. He was tall, blonde, and very handsome. I was smitten with him! I would brag to my friend that he looked just like Robert Redford (like most everyone, I had a crush on Redford for years). The first time that his hand brushed against mine, I felt a jolt of energy rush through me. We started dating and fell in love. How did I know I was in love? Because when we kissed our worlds collided. The swell of bliss would make me weep. They were tears of joy.

We were inseparable but he was unwilling to commit. The arrangement was embarrassing for me after a couple of years of him living with my family, so I persuaded him to propose. I was told by the British side of the family, that the wedding was a classy event, except for the name of the disc jockey "Funky Joe". It was a fairytale wedding with a dreamy honeymoon. But fairytales don't last and just like Cinderella, my horse-drawn carriage turned into a pumpkin at midnight. In the 2003 film, "Under the Tuscan Sun" Frances says, "I looked for it but I didn't find it – but that doesn't mean it doesn't exist?" I have come to appreciate that there are advantages to being single and married. To be single or married should strictly be a choice – not an imposition.

28 | LOSS IS INEVITABLE.

Life is about loss and the triumph of the human spirit despite it all. There is no escaping loss. We are born. We die. But in between, we live. In the 1997 film "Titanic", Jack is a free-spirited artist and third-class passenger (played by the magnificent Leonardo Di Caprio), who meets Rose, a wealthy first-class passenger (played by the beautiful Kate Winslet), as she's about to jump off the stern of the ship in third class and tries to talk her out of it. Jack says to Rose, "Don't do it." But she has made up her mind, "You're distracting me. Go away!" Jack pleads with her, "I can't. I'm involved now. You let go and I'm, I'm 'onna have to jump in there after you." And from then on their lives become entwined forever. They fall in love. When the ship is sinking and Rose jumps off the lifeboat, as it's being lowered into the ocean and onto the side of the ship, Rose runs back to Jack and tells him "You jump. I jump Jack!" A short while later, as the ship is going down, they jump into the frigid water together and hanging on for their lives Jack tells Rose, "Winning that ticket Rose was the best thing that ever happened to me. It brought me to you." With his last breath the heroic Jack rises to the human challenge and begs Rose, "You must promise me that you'll survive, that you won't give up, no matter what happens, no matter how hopeless. Promise me now, Rose, and never let go of that promise." Rose answers him, "I promise." Jack urges her, "Never let go." And Rose says, "I'll never let go Jack. I'll never let go."

Grief always follows loss like a long shadow. A loss that touches the heart is devastating. No-one else can feel your loss, no matter how generic it may be. Loss is very personal and there is no cure. The death of a loved one is one of the hardest losses that we all have to face at some point in our lives. It may be comforting to know that we do get through it eventually. That doesn't mean that the void gets filled but rather that we manage to move forward despite the loss. My first experience with loss was when my dad died. He had been sick for a long while and it was not unexpected that he would pass but that didn't diminish the hurt or make it any easier to bear. The funeral was such an elaborate ending and in stark contrast to the harsh life he endured. It made me question everything. Is the circle of life much to do about nothing? Come to think of it, funerals are a lot like weddings. (It wasn't that long ago when a wedding outfit would be saved to be worn at one's funeral.) I stood in that ominous place absolutely still, with all my senses fixed upon the casket which my sister and I had chosen for my dad. It was a laminated wooden box with elaborate golden handles covered with a spray of red roses, placed front-center before the altar. It was as if I was staring down Mortality which had just committed another cowardly act of thievery. I could have pinched myself. As long as I had known my dad, he acted the part of a sceptic. He would be amused that a blasphemous infidel like him was allowed so close to the altar of worship. My dad had a reputation for being fierce. Rumor had it that he and his beloved pair of oxen kept company with the spirits of the underworld as he crisscrossed through the mountains on many frigid nights, so he could provide for his family.

My dad was a loving father who would spoil his children whenever possible. He was also a drunk and an obstinate fool sometimes. At his core, I'm convinced he was a believer. How could it be that all that he was would simply vanish? He was too defiant to accept such a fate. Those who believe in an afterlife are comforted knowing that they will be rewarded someday for their sacrifices. The grief that followed my dad's passing overwhelmed me. I would burst into tears and throb uncontrollably, especially at night. My husband would put his arms around me and hold me tight without saying a word and this comforted me.

In life we cannot always blame our loss on an invisible force. Man played a big role in the sinking of the ill-fated Titanic and the huge loss of human life. The first time my husband told me he was leaving me it felt like a rug was pulled from under my feet. I could not imagine a life without him. He was my life! Ordinarily grief is expressed outwardly, which is healthy, but sometimes it gets buried by shame. In the 1997 film "Titanic" Rose says, "A woman's heart is an ocean of secrets." When he left for the last time the pain of the loss was unbearable and it was sustained for a long time. It wasn't any less painful just because I had endured it before.

Separation and divorce are terrible ordeals which can drag on far too long. The injury is exacerbated by blame and anger. One just cannot get on with grieving and healing because there's a big hangover. Further grievances happen and aggravate the loss. No matter how much we want to feel better we don't, until one day we do feel better. We emerge from the ashes. Time dulls the pain and eases the suffering. One can't just get over it. One must feel and process the pain, the anger, and the grief until the hurt gradually subsides. It helps if we have someone who will listen to our endless lament and stand with us when we need support. Such a person would be an angel. I have been rescued by angels more than once.

29 | SELFISHNESS AND SELF-CARE ARE ALTOGETHER DIFFERENT.

I use to get one confused with the other. Selfish people make me want to scream especially when they are inconsiderate towards others. But self-care is about taking care of ourselves and having fun. We get so distracted during our day that we often run on fumes and don't know it. I often miss the fact that I'm dying of thirst. I have to continuously remind myself that making me a priority is not the same thing as being selfish. After all, when we are happy we are fun to be around and that's good for everybody else too.

In the 2006 film "The Holiday", Kate Winslet and Cameron Diaz trade homes in different countries to escape the men who are breaking their hearts. Upon arriving in L.A., Kate gets put straight by her neighbor, the infamous screen writer played by Eli Wallach, who tells her that her problem is that she is playing the support role of the grievous friend whereas she should be the leading lady. Kate gets what he means and sobbingly says, "That's right. After all, you're supposed to be the leading lady in your own life. ... I've been going to a therapist for two years and she's never explained it to me so clearly."

We only have one chance at life and you would think that we would try to have fun with it. In the 2011 film "One Day" with Anne Hathaway and Jim Sturgess, Dexter takes his best friend Emma on a much needed holiday to France. They have a secret crush on one another and we can feel the romantic tension between them. Emma is supposedly worried that their friendship will be compromised and during the drive in his green open convertible, she insists on setting rules. "Separate bedrooms; wherever we stay no shared beds; no drunken cuddles," she says. "Well, I don't see the point of cuddling anyway. Cuddles give you cramps," he mutters. "Agreed; rule number 2: no flirting; no having a few drinks and getting frisky with me or anyone else for that matter," she says. "Well, I never flirt," he protests. And just then, they are distracted by a parade of cars driving past them. It's a wedding party. "Oh! Hello-o! What's this? Bonjour! Bon chance! Aha-ha-ha..." he yells out flirtatiously and erupts into a voluptuous laugh which takes us along for the ride. Emma quickly puts us back on track. "Which leads me to rule number 3," continues Emma, "the nudity clause." "What?" he exclaims. "I don't want to see you in the shower, or have a wee, or have a wee in the shower," she instructs. "Well, I can't promise that," he says emphatically. "You have to Dex. It's the rules," she explains, "and absolutely no skinny dipping." Dexter sounding resigned says, "alright then, rule no 4: no scrabble." "But I love scrabble," she protests. "Exactly; that's why it's my rule. Look, we're not dead yet," he tells her and parks the car. "Voila!" he says.

Nurturing ourselves makes life better. There is no conflict of interest. It's not either them or us; it's them and us. Some of us need permission to enjoy ourselves and feel we must resist any indulgence. When Dexter walks Emma to the oversized pool of water adjacent the ocean, Emma gets nervous upon realizing his intentions, and says, "Oh hello! What's going on here?" "I thought we'd go for a quick swim; sober us up," he says. "Ah... I get it. I get it. I walked right into it. Haven't I? Get a girl drunk and lead her to a large body of water." "Oh come on Emma, be spontaneous. Be reckless. Live for the moment." Dexter has to coax Emma to jump into the pool with him," "Come on Em. Come in. You're such a prude. Why are you such a prude? Come on." She scolds him, "You could have at least left your underpants on. Rule number 3, remember?" "Come on Em," he insists. And Em undresses and jumps in. "So this is skinny dipping," she says.

30 | "BELUGA IS MY BEETHOVEN," SAID THE 90-YEAR OLD BETTY WHITE...

Betty held up a photograph of her kneeling on the side of an aquarium embracing a beautiful-shiny-white beluga. The beluga was named Beethoven. Anderson had just asked her if she ever thought of marrying for a second time and it was her segue into talking about her passion for her organization whose cause was to save endangered species. She did get around to answering his question eventually, "When you've had the best you don't need the rest." How lucky for her.

Upon hearing her speak of Beethoven I had a flashback to a time when my family was endangered. On one of our "overnight" trips, we got caught in a spontaneous electrical storm. It was so frightening that my husband, who is a fantastic driver and has guided us through many downpours, pulled the car over immediately despite our need to make good time. The sky went from mid-day brightness to mid-night darkness in an instant; it was as if someone had shut the shutters to block out the sun and made the room absolutely pitch-black.

My little one was in a child car-seat, on the passenger side at the front of the car, and I was sitting in the back. We had to do something so he wouldn't be terrified. We had no idea how long this event would last. Ordinarily I had a few toys handy to amuse him on these long drives but he couldn't possibly play with toys in the dark. I reached into the diaper bag and pulled out his play-back toy recorder. One of the cassette tapes I had borrowed from the library during my last weekly visit was of Beethoven. If the truth be told we're not classical buffs and I had no idea what was on the tape. I inserted it in the recorder, pressed the play button, and raised the volume hoping to drown out the storm. The thunder was loud and furious and the lightening etched the sky violently, all of which was frightening. Astonishingly, Beethoven, not wanting to be upstaged, conducted the symphony with all the elements playing together. The arrangement was exhilarating. We laid there all three of us without a stir, enthralled by the entire spectacle. It was a private performance just for us. The sound system was tremendous. I'm sure that the arrangement gave Beethoven a bit of a stir. Eventually Beethoven put us to sleep. When we woke up, the storm had cleared and daylight had returned as if uninterrupted. We were relieved that we had come through safely and thankful to Beethoven for the performance of a lifetime. When we pulled out of our parking spot, we noticed that we had stopped next to a large petrol-storage tank. We were fortunate indeed to have had Beethoven in charge.

31 | PRUNING IS NECESSARY TO PROMOTE NEW GROWTH.

Mom would complain that dad pruned everything too harshly but he was confident in what he did. Renewal is only possible when we're ready to let go of the old in order to make room for the new. The art of pruning used to be a necessary skill passed on from one generation to the next. Similarly the art of living frugally was learned in the home. But the boomer generation skipped that lesson because boomers arrived during a period of tremendous economic expansion. (I'm a boomer.) In contrast, our parents grew up with scarcity, depression, and wars, and consequently suffered tremendously. They wanted to spare us their suffering and in their zeal ended up spoiling most of us.

In the 2011 film "From Prada to Nada" (a Latin twist on Jane Austen's "Sense and Sensibility") Nora (played by Camilla Belle) is a law student who is socially awkward and her sister Mary (played by Alex Vega) is a spoiled rich kid who loves to party. They live an affluent lifestyle at Casa Bonita with their loving father, having lost their mother. Mary walks inside her mansion and sees some Mexican workers and says, "What is this? Tijuana?" It's their father's birthday and when he enters the scene, he twirls his girls about in a dance but suffers a heart attack and dies. They then learn that he was bankrupt and at his funeral discover they have a half-brother who is married to a greedy and evil woman. After having to sell their interest in their beautiful mansion to their half-brother, they get kicked out by their sister-in-law who says, "We have the house but can't keep the orphans that came with it."

They are taken in by their maternal aunt Aurelia (played by Adriana Barraza), who lives on the East side of L.A. On their way there, Mary says to Nora, "I'm really scared right now, Nora. Like we're gonna get shot," and Mary tries to calm her down, "Would you just calm down. This place is perfectly safe," and someone says, "Welcome to barrio, mija," and Mary is scared, "Drive. Just drive. Oh my God." Later Aunt Aurelia tells us a bit about the 'hood, "This place used to be Jewish, then Japanese and then Latino," and Mary sarcastically says, "It's totally Calcutta except it's less hot and there's a breeze."

Upon arriving at their aunt's house, the next-door neighbor Bruno (played by Wilmer Valderrama), a rough-looking younger man with long hair, tattoos, and working clothes, helps them with their luggage. Mary bumps into him as she struts past him in her 3-inch heels and ironically says, "Are you homeless," and Bruno replies, "No. Are you?" Bruno turns out to be a talented artist and caring person. Their aunt is working class and has illegal immigrants in her home sewing to make a living. She quickly sells Mary's Boomer and Prada purse and buys her an old used vehicle and says, "Don't worry. It will take you to the same place." Their new life is a far cry from what they were used to and they miss their parents. Nora is willing to make the best of the situation and wants to be helpful. When Nora tries to fry some eggs, her aunt tells her, "Careful. Last two eggs. How is it possible that you don't know the basics," and Nora says, "Do you know how to fly a plane," and her aunt answers, "Of course not. Why should I," and Nora tells her, "Right. Well, because you never had to. I never had to cook. I'm willing to learn," and her aunt says, "Learn to clean. Then we go out for a little desayuno," "Not downtown," and the aunt says, "No its worse. East L.A."

Nora decides to quit school and take a job as a Law Clerk while Mary goes back to school to get her diploma. When Mary drops Nora off at the bus stop, she says, "Here's your bus. Don't sit at the back. You'll get killed," and Nora asks, "By whom? A commuter?" They say good bye and Mary adds, "Oh my God. We have joined the working class. Lame!" Mary falls head over heels with her English professor's T.A. and believes that he is her ticket out of the working class. She tells him, "I love poetry, pasta, and Prada." As the plot unwinds, she discovers that he is a two-timing phony who buys her family mansion for his wife and not for her; unlike what she had chosen to believe. She learns to see past the clothes and through the superficial charm and appreciate Bruno's authentic and sensitive personality. Nora tries to resist Edward's (played by Nicholas Agosto) advances towards her, her sister-in-law's brother and her boss, who has been courting her since they first met at the beginning of the film. In the end, she accepts his love and they marry and go into business together as Legal Counsels in their new community.

Most of us don't live in mansions but we wish we did! The boomer generation grew up wanting to live life large. We don't like to defer so we use credit. Western nations have racked up a lot of debt during the past thirty years or so. The hole is so enormous that it's causing world economies to implode – austerity is the new buzz word now. The day has come to pay the piper, and as it happens, everyone will share in the pain. My parents always paid for everything with cash. Sometimes we compromised and other times we did without. We were poor but not in the hole. We never minded not getting Christmas gifts – it was not our custom. We celebrated Christmas for the birth of Jesus and then waited anxiously for the Epiphany on the 6th of January, which is when the Magi visited Baby Jesus. That's when "La Befana" (the good witch from the North dressed in dark rags and a stained apron, and blackened by ashes) who undoubtedly was very ugly, travelled on her broomstick during the night time to get to children's homes. She would enter through the chimney and leave presents behind. The next morning I would rush excitedly to locate the sock, which had been hung mysteriously on the staircase the night before. I sat on the staircase with my sisters huddled around me, reached into the sock and pulled out an orange or a tangerine and some chocolate and candy. If we had been really good during the year we might have found one or two special sweets called "torrone" – a sugary concoction of chocolate-covered hazelnuts. It had an exquisite wrapper. I was enormously satisfied. As I got a little older I suspected that the treats and tangerines might have come off the Christmas tree. That's when I considered that the sock was old and probably my dad's. I guessed that what we got had more to do with availability than being good. We were ecstatic nonetheless with our goodies from La Befana and shared them happily with family. There is no denying that "less is more". The gift was in the anticipation.

Kids today want all the latest gadgets. Parents start out wanting to stick to a budget but cannot resist giving their children what they ask for. We all feel entitled to having what everybody else has. But come January we have to grapple with how to pay the credit card bill. You never save when you buy stuff, even if it's on sale or on a payment plan. It's always a transfer of your wealth to the retailer. You can't spend your way into prosperity. Pruning our desires and editing our wish list is necessary in order for us to afford what we really need in the present as well as the future. I find it not very funny that some people can't pay their monthly rent or hydro bill and risk being put out on the street, yet they have to have cable and cell phones. Apparently the children also need cell phones. If we don't save on the discretionary stuff we won't be able to afford what we really need. The saying "pennies from heaven" is a clever way of telling us to hang on to our small change. It adds up. Just look at all the earnings banks accumulate from service fees. It takes discipline and determination to become debt-free and prosperous. A well-pruned lifestyle will help us live our best life.

32 | ARE YOU A BIG PRANKSTER?

Maybe you are more of a comedian? Pranksters, tricksters, and goofs are an unappreciated bunch but they usually make us laugh. Most of us have a deep longing for laughter. It's relief for the spirit and the best medicine for the body. My favorite pass time is a light-hearted sit-com or a romantic-comedy film. I used to be a big fan of "Everybody Loves Raymond" along with everybody else. It was my mom's favorite as well and she understood it without speaking the language. During her last years, it was one of her few pastimes as she was mostly bedridden. I'd turn to the re-runs regularly to distract her from her aches and pains. Watching the same episode over again was like wearing a favorite sweater. Her face would light up as if she was in the company of friends and she would smile inwardly at the familiar gestures and jokes.

My son's favorite sit-com used to be a toss-up between "Two-and-a-half Men" and "The Simpsons", both of which were on his dad's X List. Nowadays he gets most of his laughs from "YouTube". I don't think he recalls the time when we sat together in the evening as a family to watch "Home Improvement". The original stand-up comedy of Tim Taylor which poked fun at men and their "piggish" habits and Tim's skill as a prankster made the series a big hit. Recently I caught an old Victor Borge special on the Public TV Network and was amazed by his enormous talent. I had forgotten him. Few people know who Borge was but he is undoubtedly deserving of resurgence. Borge was an extraordinarily successful entertainer in the 1960's with a great life story. He was a Danish comedian, conductor, and pianist who fled the Nazis and arrived in the States penniless. It was said that he was the funniest and highest paid entertainer (according to the New York Times) of his day. He could make you laugh without saying a word much like "The Three Stooges" did with their pranks. The old silent pictures were hysterical and it appears that they're making a comeback. This year's Academy Award for best film went to none other than "The Artist" – a silent picture. Everything old is new again – eventually.

I wish I was funny but most of the time I can't even remember a joke. Occasionally I write one down if I'm really keen to share it. I really enjoy smartly-scripted jokes in romantic-comedy films, like "Under the Tuscan Sun". In one scene, where Marcello is racing on a winding road which traces the edge of a cliff – a precipice overlooking a spectacular view of the Mediterranean – Francesca asks him, "Do traffic lights mean anything around here?" Marcello replies, "Yeah, sure. Green light – avanti, avanti! Yellow light – decoration." Francesca can't resist the follow-up question, "And what about red light?" Marcello answers, "Just a suggestion!"

In an interview, Anderson Cooper was talking to the infamous Betty While about proper etiquette with mountain guerrillas. He explained that when visiting with mountain guerrillas, which he has done over 30 times, you're never supposed to stand taller than them. But when one of the fellows with him stood up without thinking, the mountain guerrilla simply stretched out its arm over the fellow's head and lowered him. Anderson stretched out his arm to imitate the guerrilla as he told the story. You really had to be there!

Most of us take ourselves much too seriously and have lost the ability to play and have fun. The pranksters I've known were labelled school clowns and goofs. They would write something on the blackboard or change the seating arrangement while the teacher was out of the room. It was harmless fun and everybody would get a chuckle out of it, except the teacher perhaps. It woke everybody up and provided comic relief in an otherwise monotonous (boring) classroom. Injecting humor into our lives is necessary and not difficult to do.

Jerry Seinfeld told Anderson that he liked to be funny at home with his kids and not just on stage. He and his children liked to poke fun at visitors. They each would take turns imitating something about their friends as they were leaving, for example their walk. Having fun with your family is precious. My sister's boys would prank their mother at every chance while growing up and still do. They would drink from her glass when she wasn't looking or sneak up behind her and give her a scare. I would challenge my toddler to keep a straight face while I contorted mine and then he would challenge me. Within seconds we would burst out laughing. Who could resist such clowning and silliness? More than anything, he liked to be tickled and "TickeFingers" would almost always oblige.

It is apparent that laughter is a popular pastime. "YouTube" is a goldmine of humorous clips posted by amateur want-a-be comedians and pranksters, some of whom get millions of views. Email though is another story. Thankfully the "spam" folder spares us from some not-so-funny jokes.

33 | MY CHILD HAS ALWAYS BEEN ENAMORED WITH CATS AND DOGS.

When Tiger was only a baby, I was taken aback with how he gravitated to cats and dogs without any hesitation. It was unnerving. My sister had a king-size German Sheppard named Sheba and he adored it. After Sheba, there was Cleo. Tiger cherished all the time he spent with them. I was delighted that he got so much pleasure without me being saddled with the responsibilities of owning a pet. The short-term visits were a win-win for everybody. On one visit, when Tiger was about three-and-half years old, we couldn't find him anywhere in the house. When we ran out to look for him, we found him coming around the bend. He had taken Sheba for a walk or was it the other way around? When Sheba had to be put down, it was very sad for everybody. Tiger was still a toddler when we were asked to dog sit the pup Cleo for a week. One day Cleo got its head caught in the chicken-wire fence in our back yard. Tiger skillfully rescued it all by himself, and luckily saved Cleo's eye. It bonded him to Cleo even more, if that were possible. He was proud of himself and so was I.

I always approach a dog with trepidation. That's because when I was about six I got bitten. That was my second encounter with a dog. The first time was when I saw one with its head in a noose, hanging from a tree. Apparently the dog had eaten someone's chickens and had to be put down. That was the way then. On the day that I got bitten, I was hanging out with my teen sisters while they cultivated crops. It was a hot day and they asked me to fetch some water. The spring water couldn't have been very far but I dreaded the chore. I felt tense just being there. That parcel of land was next to the cemetery and being in those surroundings gave me the creeps. I had to walk the entire length of the cemetery stone-wall, across the road, and through the next field to get to the water. I hastened my pace once I crossed the road and listened intensely for any stir that any soul might make. It was their sacred ground. As I crossed the field I heard barking in the distance. It seemed to come from an old shed to my left. I scurried on and was making my way back when I was jumped by a huge beast that I never saw coming. I could hear my sister screaming at it trying to scare the dog off while she ran towards me, and the incident was over in a minute. Except that in those days, any bite from an animal that lived in the wild carried the risk of rabies and I was old enough to understand and worry about that. As it happened, this dog's bite was on account of its natural instinct to protect its litter. I have sympathy with the animal but my scar is a constant reminder of the wild side to all creatures.

34 | ARGUMENTS ARE LIKE BAD WEATHER: UNPREDICTABLE AND UNWELCOME.

Everyone knows that light rain can quickly change to a downpour. No matter how hard you try not to get wet, it's unavoidable. Often we allow grievances to fester because we are unable to talk about our feelings. We focus too much on what someone did wrong rather than expressing how it made us feel. Dr. Phil likes to say that every pancake has two sides. An argument usually erupts because we only want to see one side. When there is pent-up anger or hurt feelings, any comment can spark an argument. A sharp tongue or a sensitive nerve will cause the argument to escalate. When an argument spirals into a screaming match or into name calling, the brew is toxic. No good can come of it. It is best to leave the room as soon as the volume goes up. The more we are riled up the less will be resolved.

To really know what one may be thinking you need to see their eyes. My dad mistrusted anyone who did not look at him straight in the eyes when they spoke. If we cannot speak our truth with kind words than we might as well be invisible. Invisible people drift apart. When two people can speak to one another softly, honestly, and clearly they can bridge the gap between them. If they cannot be transparent the gap grows. When there is disagreement, it is always best to begin a statement with "I..." Talking about feelings rather than who's right and who's wrong is constructive. For example, "When you did that, it made me feel like I didn't matter to you." Sometimes we can communicate our feelings about a problem or an issue better with a note or an email. Other times we need a mediator to resolve the issue. When we hurl insults and resort to name calling we're on a slippery path. If we are arguing because we want the pleasure of being told that "we are right" or if we feel the urge to embarrass or diminish the other person, then the war is lost.

While we may not want seasons to change, they do anyway. Sometimes we live with our illusions and delusions because it's the only way we can cope. Trouble may come when you least expect it but the clues were there all along. Trust is built on transparency not opaqueness. If we are forever compromising or feeling like something is missing (respect, intimacy, connectedness) then a storm is brewing. We all want to be respected. When we feel like we're being stepped on, anger builds. If we are too flexible or have porous boundaries we are vulnerable. It's like putting out a doormat that says "go ahead and step on me". If you don't stand up for yourself, the world will knock you over. Being "too nice" is a clue that we are trying too hard to please others. We are afraid of rejection.

In the 2011 film "Something Borrowed" Rachel (played by Ginnifer Goodwin) and Darcy (played by Kate Hudson) have been inseparable and best friends since elementary school. The friendship is crushed when Rachel and Dex (played by Collin Egglesfield) sleep together just before Dex is to marry Darcy. In law school, Dex was Rachel's study partner and they had feelings for each other but never got the nerve to let the other know about it. When Rachel invited her best friend to join her and Dex for lunch, the sexually confident and outspoken Darcy hit on Dex and they became romantically involved after that. All the while Rachel continued to have feelings for Dex and suffered secretly as she watched him be with her best friend. Now she's Darcy's maid of honor and even writes her vows. The friends supposedly tell each other everything. Neither Rachel or Dex have the nerve to tell Darcy the truth – they don't want to hurt her supposedly. In one scene Rachel says to her best friend Darcy, "When do I ever say No to you?" Ethan (played by John Krasinski) has a crush on Rachel and finds out about the entanglement. He tries to persuade Rachel to speak up, "I don't get how you let her win. You yield to her at every turn... Why," and Rachel answers, "Because that's what Darcy does. She gets things." In the end Rachel realizes that she got it wrong and finds the courage to tell Dex she wants him, "I always thought it was Darcy that took you. It was me just giving," and, "I just didn't think that someone like you could like someone like me." But Dex loves Rachel and they finally get together. The funny thing is that Darcy had to discover the truth by chance. Rachel and Darcy's friendship is lost even though Darcy never really wanted Dex anyway. Months later when Darcy bumps into Rachel, Darcy says to her, "I'm happy." There is a time to be bold and confident. When you're fair and firm, the world will come around.

35 | WEDDINGS ARE BEAUTIFUL.

We all want to believe in the Cinderella story. The wedding of Charles, Prince of Wales to Lady Diana Frances Spencer, captivated the imagination of a billion people around the world. The royal wedding took place on Wednesday, 29th of July, 1991. Britain declared the day a national holiday. Fast forward to Friday, 29th of April, 2011, and the royal wedding of Prince William, Duke of Cambridge to Kate Middleton was even more of a fairytale. It was the true Cinderella story – a wedding of a commoner to a prince.

We all want the fairytale and are determined to make it happen at least for one day. A wedding is a super-sized confectionary of fashion, flowers, food, family, friends, and fantasy. An invitation to attend a wedding nowadays is a sign of esteem, especially if you are not closely related to the bride and groom. Weddings have become exclusive events due to their skyrocketing production costs. I was lucky enough to be invited to a wedding in Hawaii recently. It was a long-overdue reunion with my beloved friend from Japan. It was the smallest and most exquisite wedding I've ever attended. I remember when the guest list would easily include 400 people – everyone that the parents knew was invited to the happy event. Weddings are always elaborate and lavish, regardless of how rich or poor everyone is. When we are on the guest list, participating in such a grand event is a special treat. There is so much pomp and ceremony.

The wedding ceremony is the first act in a magical day which is so full of hope and promise. The guests wait with bated breath for the moment when the lucky bride appears on her daddy's arm, determined to begin the royal procession towards her prince charming. He is standing expectantly at the opposite end, separated by what seems like a long mile. Everyone is captivated by the entire spectacle of flowers and fashions and faces. The anxious guests try to shuffle their feet quietly as they shift their gaze between the bride and the groom. The vision of the virgin bride draped in heaps of lace and ruffles is mesmerizing but her visage is blurred by a long veil.

In contrast, the groom stands erect in a black tux with only hints of white, sporting a single bud on his lapel. His face is charmingly transparent and there is no mistaking his nervous pose. When the first solemn note of the wedding hymn is played, there's a big sigh. It's the bride's cue to start her march. Every step she takes is intentional. When she reaches the altar, her daddy raises the veil and presents his darling daughter to her suitor. They smile at one another and proceed to face the official who is charged to bless the union. He speaks to them about love and its obligations and tribulations before segueing into the scripted contract. As we listen to the familiar clauses we are personally moved and filled with longing. Our thoughts are interrupted as the bride and groom exchange vows and rings to show their unwavering commitment. The official then pronounces that they are man and wife and the groom leans forward to give his bride a kiss and seal their union. Every minute of the joyous event is captured on video and photographed. The celebration continues into the midnight hour when the happy couple is finally able to escape and be alone.

A flash back to my childhood in Italy conjures up a vision of an entirely different scene which I witnessed personally. Alas there's no other record. It is Sunday morning and a beautiful bride walks hand in hand with her groom to the steeple church just up the road from my house. Church bells are ringing perpetually. They are followed closely behind by a flock of family and friends. Her bridal dress is straight-cut satin and simple lace. It's custom and beautifully made but not a designer label imported from a distant couture shop. It was most likely borrowed from a family member or friend, as were the wedding bands.

There is much laughter and happiness in the air which has an enchanted fragrance. There's a carpet of flower petals on the cobblestone pavement. Children volunteered earlier that morning to unravel the flowers which had been picked in the fields the day before. They are charged with tossing the petals all along the promenade which stretches from the bride's parents' home to the church. Everyone is carried away with excitement but not hurried. There is no risk of being late since everyone is present and participating. The wedding ceremony lasts a while. It follows a Catholic Mass sung in Old Latin and ends with the Benediction of the happy couple and all the witnesses.

When the bride and groom finally emerge on the church steps, a gaggle of children encircle them, anxious to grab the coins which will be tossed any second up high into the air by family members showering the couple with ringing wishes of prosperity.

Everyone strolls back to the couple's new home to enjoy liqueurs and home-made cookies, cioccolatini, and confetti (hard-sugar-coated almonds). The house is theirs outright, land title and all, a gift from the bride's parents. She also brings a dowry. The furnishings are a gift from the grooms' parents. The celebration will continue for days and weeks to come, when friends and family will visit them, bearing gifts in over-sized baskets lined with the nicest hand-embroidered linen. Their pantry will be well supplied with necessities to last the happy couple several seasons. In return, the bride will put some wedding treats in the basket and cover them with the same linen that lined it originally, before taking it back to their family member or friend.

The 2012 film "The Vow" is a modern-day love story of how "true love" conquers all. It was filmed in Chicago and Toronto and was "inspired by true events" based on the love story of Kim and Krickitt Carpenter. Leo Collins (played by Channing Tatum), a musician, meets Page Thornton (played by Rachel McAdams), a student artist, in a line-up for a Residential Parking Permit and asks her out. The courtship is a whirlwind romance and after only two weeks Page is in love with Leo. He asks her to move in and they get married shortly thereafter. The wedding ceremony is performed in a room at the Art Gallery of Chicago. The bride and groom, and about a dozen of their closest eclectic friends sneak in to the venue. The vows they make to one another are words that pull at our heart-strings. Page reads off a menu from their favorite café , "I vow to help you love life, to always hold you with tenderness and to have the patience that love demands, to speak when words are needed and to share the silence when they are not and to live within the warmth of your heart and always call it home." Then Leo speaks, "Well...You set the bar kind of high... Did you write your vows on a menu? [He pulls out the same menu leaflet.] ...I vow to fiercely love you in all your forms, now and forever. I promise to never forget that this is a once in a lifetime love. I vow to love you, and no matter what challenges might carry us apart, we will always find a way back to each other."

Ten weeks later they're in a car accident and Page loses all memory of Leo and the last five years of her life. When she wakes up in the hospital she doesn't recognize him at all and has no recollection of their life together. Leo needs to persuade Page to go home with him, but Page is lost – she's trapped in the past. She remembers only being in law school and being engaged to Jeremy. Leo pleads with her, "Page. Okay... Babe. Babe. Just...The best thing to do at this point is to go back with your life with me. You heard what the doctor said. It's the best thing for your recovery," but she argues, "Okay... but I don't know you and I'm just supposed to get into your car and go and live at your place," and Leo says, "It's our place." Page is not convinced, "Without any proof of us even being in love," and Leo tells her, "Other than our marriage?" Page argues, "People get married for all kinds of different reasons," and Leo says in disbelief, "Like?" and Page answers, "Like for a green card." Leo tells her, "I'm from Cincinnati," and Page asks, "Did I keep a journal?" "No. Not that I know of," he answers. Page shakes her head and says, "I..." and walks away.

But Leo will not give up on their marriage, "I need to make my wife fall in love with me again." Leo drives to Lake Forrest, where she's now living with her parents, to attend her sister's engagement party. He spots her in the doorway coming out to the garden – a Royal-Doulton version of his bride, and exclaims, "Page ...," and she says, "Hey. Hi Leo," perplexed by his look of surprise. Leo says, "Your hair. It looks so different. You look beautiful." As if he were a stranger she says, "Thank you." Leo resumes, "Okay, hey look. I've been thinking about something," and Page says, "Okay." Leo starts, "What's your favorite book?" Page wonders what he's getting at and says "Ah... It's probably not what you remember," and Leo says, "That's fine. That's not the point." Page tells him, "The Beachhouse by James Patterson," and Leo says, "Na. Really?" Page says, "Yaa." Leo proceeds, "Okay. The Beachouse. Well, if it was great you probably loaned it to somebody," and Page answers, "Ya. Gwen I think." Leo says, "and you probably said to yourself, 'I wish I was the person that hadn't read it so that I could experience it all over again,'" and Page nods, "Ya. I guess so." Leo goes on, "Well, that's how I think we should look at this." But Page doesn't get it, "Ah? What," and Leo explains, "You can't remember how we met and you can't remember how we fell in love and in a way ya, that sucks. But it was the greatest time in my life and I just thought how cool it would be to get to experience it all over again. Page gets it, "Like reading your favorite book for the first time," and Leo says, "Exactly," and Page nods, "Gotcha." Leo makes his move, "Which is why I want to ask you out on a date," and Page looks perplexed, "A date?" Leo explains, "Like two people that are just meeting for the first time." Page shifts her gaze to her former fiancée and says, "A date? ... Ah... Well, I don't know. You know, got the wedding coming up," and Leo tries to convince her, "But if we go out before then you might still be able to take me as your date. I can't promise anything but I'll put in a good word for you." Page gives in, "Alright... a date."

When Leo goes to pick up Page, he asks her if she's okay with them going into the city, and she answers, "Ya. That's fine. I just have to be back by 10 in the morning." Leo teases her, "Oh my God. First date and you're already inviting yourself to spend the night," and while she tries to clarify, he teases some more, "I know. I'm just a little scandalized. That's all." Leo takes Page to the exact parking spot where they met the first time and says, "I'm going to take you on a little retrospective of us." The date convinces Leo that they still belong together but thereafter he succumbs to all the pressures, "I give up... if we were meant to be, we would be together," and agrees to a divorce. As it turns out their fate is for them to be together. All it takes is time. Without ever regaining her memory, Page is drawn back to the life she had with Leo, "It's crazy what my hands remember that my mind forgot," she tells him in the final scene, and then, "Thank you." Leo says to her, "I didn't do anything," and she tearfully tells him, "You did everything. You accepted me for who I am and not for what you wanted me to be," and an emotional Leo says, "I just wanted you to be happy. That's all."

36 | HOLIDAYS ARE DESSERT.

They are delectable and delicious and unless we indulge too much, relatively risk-free. On holidays most businesses are closed and workers get a respite from their day-to-day grind. "Holy" days are sprinkled throughout the year to celebrate Christmas, Easter, and Thanksgiving among others. While we look forward to holidays, the time is usually committed, over-booked, and brief. We want more time. We want "free" time. That means vacation. A vacation is intended to be restorative, thrilling, and salacious. Most of us secretly believe we are entitled to a vacation annually.

While it may seem incredulous, our ancestors worked every day without ever taking a vacation. I heard it put this way, "I've never been anywhere but here". Few of us can afford a vacation every year. We cannot afford to "throw" money on a "perk" when there are more pressing needs that have priority over family funds. There is the kids' education, car repairs, and lots of loans – car loans, equity loans, credit card loans, … If we are lucky, we get one vacation to mark a major milestone. It may be a honeymoon or we may have to wait for retirement.

In the 2011 film "One Day", Dexter, (played by Jim Sturgess), takes Emma (played by Anne Hathaway) on a "magical" vacation to France on their anniversary – 15th of July 1992. On one of their first evenings there, while enjoying an intimidate chat and a bottle of wine outdoors at their retreat, Emma says to Dexter, "Do you know I've never been abroad," and Dexter in disbelief answers, "What? Don't be ridiculous." Emma says, "It's true. A fortnight in a caravan in

Whitby drinking a cup of soup with dad and trying not to kill mom... I can't believe I'm actually here with you."

I've been lucky. I was 21 when I went overseas to Europe with my sister and my mom. The rail in Europe is amazing for travelers and tourists. We boarded the train in Amsterdam and made numerous stops through Germany and Italy. It was the first and only time that my mom saw St. Peter's Cathedral, the Leaning Tower of Pisa, the Grand Canals in Venice, and the Palazzo Vecchio in Florence. She lived in Italy half of her life and yet had never visited any of these beautiful places.

Those who travel for work sometimes have an opportunity to explore places they would not otherwise visit. My first job took me to Hawaii and San Francisco and who could complain about that. I returned to the tropical paradise a couple of months later for a three-week vacation with my sister and best friend. The trip to Hawaii had been planned before I knew I was to go there on business. It was an adventure which gave us thrill and leisure, but more importantly, memories to last a lifetime. Like the day we set out to drive around the island of Maui without researching the terrain. The road was narrow, winding, and perched on the cliff edge, along the coast. We were taken aback by frequent warnings of falling rocks. It was funny at first. The scenic route (the only route) would weave and turn and lead us through these one-way snares where there was no way of seeing around the bend. To add to the thrill, when we stopped to look at a scenic waterfall we were jolted by an earthquake. I would not be exaggerating if I said we were nervous. As the daylight disappeared and the paved road ended, we were forced to make our way back along the same treacherous path, except this time we had the outer edge the entire way. We were relieved to get back safe and sound and grateful for having purchased accident insurance.

Vacations are supposed to be the ultimate antidote to stress, but more often than not, vacations increase stress. Holidays on the other hand are predictably sweet and always a treat.

37 | I DISCOVERED THRIFT STORES WAY TOO LATE.

It's like going to the fair. There is so much to get excited about. You can find vintage, dress-up, glitter, funky, elegant, and opulent. A rare find is like winning the lottery. If happiness is the pursuit of purposefulness than thrift stores should become ubiquitous.

One person's trash is another person's treasure. A thrift store is a place where you can distract yourself for a couple of hours. It is thrilling to find an item which reminds you of your past. You can laugh at those items that are whimsical and different. You can find the one-of-a-kind plate that got broken and is missing from your china set. It's even possible to discover items that will allow you to complete a valuable collection.

When my baby was born I was lucky to have generous family that kept on giving. His paternal grandmother knitted the cutest baby outfits. His aunts bought him the latest baby fashions, accessories, and toys. At the time our finances were strained and we had little money for consumption. Every mother knows that children grow out of clothes very quickly just when they get dirty the most. I felt very lucky when a couple of my friends passed on clothing that their children had outgrown. Had I known about thrift stores, it would have given me options for dressing my child fashionably without having to scrimp and save.

My first visit to a thrift store was thrilling. I couldn't believe all the racks of lightly worn fashions which would have cost a fortune in a retail outlet. There were so many great books and toys to amuse Tiger with. Now that I see how many new outfits I have in my closet that no longer fit me, I understand how they get their fine inventory. I think of a thrift store as a major outlet that sells designer labels at bargain-basement prices.

In the 2005 film "The Sisterhood of the Travelling Pants" four teens who are best girlfriends – Lena, Tibby, Bridget, and Carmen (played by Alexis Bledel, Amber Tamblyn, Blake Lively, and Tiger Whitford) are about to separate for the summer when they decide to go browsing at a thrift store. They convince Tibby to try on a pair of jeans and are so impressed that they all have to try them on. The pants fit all of them perfectly even though they have different measurements and they decide to buy them and share them equally over the summer. At the beginning of the film, Carmen in a voiceover tells us, "It would be easy to say that the pants changed everything that summer. But looking back now I feel like our lives changed because they had to and that the real magic of the pants was in bearing witness to all this and in somehow holding us together when it felt like nothing would ever be the same again." Lena travels to Greece to visit her grandparents and finds love. She's sitting on the dock drawing when she falls in the water and the pants get caught on something. She's rescued by Kostas (played by Michael Rady), a Greek-American like her. Lena says to Kostas, "You don't even know me," and he answers, "But I'm trying to. Can't you see that?"

Tibby is working at a discount department store when a young girl faints in the deodorant isle. Tibby runs to help her and as the girl is being taken on a stretcher to the hospital, Tibby says to her, "You have a price sticker on your forehead." Later when Lena sends the pants to Tibby at the wrong house, they get delivered to her by none other than Bailey (played by Jenna Boyd), the girl she helped. Bailey becomes fascinated with Tibby's movie-making and appoints herself as her assistant. Tibby finds out that Bailey has leukemia and is dying. When she visits her in the hospital she says, "I bought something for you... tad da," and Baily says, "The Traveling Pants." Tibby explains, "Yeah, I just got them back from Lena," and Bailey asks, "The one in Greece," and Tibby answers, "Yeah, she said that we were right all along and that the pants are magic and I don't know the details but I do know Lena and for her to say that means... that it must be true... so I was thinking that maybe you could have them for a while." Baily tells Tibby the obvious, "They don't fit me, remember," and Tibby tearfully says, "Yeah, I know, but that doesn't matter... none of it really matters. You have to take them, Baily. Okay? You have to let them help you. Please. I know that you're tired, okay, but you can't give up. The pants will give you a miracle. You have to believe." Bailey answers Tibby, "The pants have already worked their magic on me. They brought me to you."

Bridget goes to a soccer camp in Baja California, Mexico, where she becomes infatuated with the coach and is single-minded about having a fling with him. (She has lost her mother to suicide and is struggling with a mood disorder.) When the pants arrive from Tibby, she puts them on and spends the night with the coach. Losing her virginity leaves Bridget feeling empty and listless.

Carmen goes to see her estranged father in North Carolina and learns that he is about to get remarried into an Anglo-Saxon Protestant family. Carmen was raised by her Puerto Rican mother. When she feels snubbed by the family, she finds the courage to return back home. Later, Carmen's friends convince her to confront her father and he ends up making a public apology to Carmen at his wedding. The pair of jeans is the link to the stories which the girlfriends share and the color to their experiences. Throughout their emotional ups and downs they are there for one another. Tibby says, "The magic is unsanitary!"

I can feel wealthy shopping at a thrift store. The selection is great and the prices are always discounted. It doesn't bother me in the least that the items are used. I am grateful that someone has gone to the trouble of sorting through their over-stocked closet and arranged for items to be picked up or delivered to a thrift store. Some people feel ashamed to disclose the source of their great finds. I guess they don't want anyone to know that they like a bargain too. Depending on our spin, anything can become trendy and perfectly acceptable. Times change and so does the discourse. Before the recession everyone liked to rave about their designer-label items; now the trend is no-name and budget. What may be old to you is new to me. Holding a party with friends and swapping each other's clothes is a cocktail of pleasure and style. Playing dress-up with our children with the vintage clothing we found at a thrift store is great fun. Attending a function in a designer-label dress that cost a fraction of the original price tag makes me feel like a million bucks.

38 | DANCE IS ABOUT CONNECTEDNESS AND RELATIONSHIPS ARE A DANCE.

Just when you've settled on a tune that you think you'll enjoy, a stranger inserts a coin in the old jukebox and selects a new song. They grab your hand and spin you around on the dance floor. Within minutes, you're squeezed by a crowd and have to tighten your step. You seem to have rhythm together and try a slow dance next. You don't want the night to end and commit to partnering long term. But after a while your dance has become monotonous and you realize that you prefer to rock while he prefers to tango. Your children tune you both out. They're into rap.

Life is a dance which is not choreographed for us. The music changes constantly and our dance becomes even more challenging. If we are willing we can keep on dancing but we have to train hard to stay nimble and flexible. Sometimes we fall down or step on each other's toes. Ideally we want our relationships to be great but life gets complicated. We may not be well matched or we may have been given two left feet.

Everyone wants the warmth that flows from connectedness. We need it. Mary J. Blige sums it up this way, "You need someone to love you. You need someone to hold you… You need someone to tell you that everything is all right." So how do you know when you've met the right person? It's like getting in a warm bath. You just know. Whenever we hear of a couple that's been together for half a century or so, we want to know how they did it. Surely they have a secret? They must have a tip or a magic trick up their sleeve. But no

109

secrets or tricks are revealed. They'll tell you that they too went through some rough patches and it was hard work. Maybe they were each other's best friend or they made each other laugh.

In the 2011 film "W.E." co-written and directed by Madonna, Wally Winthrop (played by Abbie Cornish) is fascinated by the love story of Wallis Simpson (played by Andrea Riseborough) and King Edward VIII (played by James D'Arcy). Wally is obsessed and nostalgic for the romantic dream and undying love that she believes Simpson had with Edward. In the story Edward is "possessed" by Simpson, an American divorcee who is carefree and smart. Simpson is portrayed with clarity of life which is lacking in Wally. Simpson says to Edward in a toast, "To love and other disasters!" and to her friend, "Darling, don't rain on my parade". Simpson's dance amuses Edward till the very end when she dances the twist for him as he lies in bed dying. The film weaves back and forth between Wally's empty marriage in New York in 1998 and the breakdown of the romance between Simpson and David – King Edward – following his abdication and exile in 1936. Wally has conversations with the ghost of Simpson throughout the film. In one scene, Simpson's ghostly voice tells the abused Wally, "Darling, they can't hurt you unless you let them. At the end Wally asks Simpson, "Do you think we can change our destiny," and Simpson answers, "You know the answer to that."

The more relationships we have, the harder it gets to negotiate each one. We may be better at it if we grew up with good role models. It doesn't help to be passive aggressive or just plain inconsiderate. Sometimes the children in our lives will yell, scream, taunt, and cry, and all we can do is ignore them. Sometimes there's a big glitch in our dance routine. What I've noticed is that in those families where there is connectedness there is ordered chaos. Where there is none, it's more like a circus. Those who are connected dance with each other and not around one another. They don't walk on egg shells. Families that are "connected" have unspoken rules, like transparency and accountability. For example, they call one another often just to touch base or advise of their whereabouts. Staying connected doesn' offend their sensibilities. Independence and connectedness are often confused.

Relationships are dynamic. My mother and I had a great

relationship towards the end of her life but when I was young we butted heads. I learned a lot from her during those later years when she was so ill. I learned that criticism is grinding while appreciation is uplifting. I learned to be patient and not to sweat the small stuff. I learned that life is precious and none of our possessions hold value for us in the end. I learned that to be in a relationship you have to be kind, you have to be loyal, and you have to be there. I learned to make time to dance alone while keeping one hand free.

39 | CELEBRATIONS ARE THE HIGHLIGHTS OF OUR LIVES.

Celebrations are markers for the milestones and traditions that color our past. They become fond memories that last forever. We have to make the most of any occasion that gives us reason to cheer. A wedding anniversary is a romantic milestone and a feat to be celebrated. Sometimes we make excuses to avoid celebrations. Cynics will argue that Christmas Day and Valentine's Day and Halloween are too commercial. As we get older, we don't feel like celebrating another birthday. Weddings have become too expensive and couples don't last anyway. Can you imagine the world without Christmas or birthdays or weddings? Celebrations are meant to enrich our lives – not impoverish us. It's a philosophy worth embracing. Life is too short and by the time we catch on, it may be too late. Tears of wisdom are always wet.

The 2011 film, "The Lost Valentine" is a poignant story about timeless love and the enduring spirit which never gives up. A TV journalist, Susan Allison (played by Jennifer Love Hewitt) is assigned to produce a story for airing on Valentine's Day. At first she thinks it to be a fluff piece but later becomes personally committed. Caroline Thomas (played by Betty White) has been going to the railroad station on Valentine's Day at the same time punctually for the last 66 years. That's when she said good bye to her husband, Naval Aviator Lt. Neil Thomas (played by Billy Magnussen), as he departed for the Pacific to fight in World War II. Valentine's Day was the couple's first anniversary, "We didn't go anywhere for a honeymoon," says the older Caroline as they flash back to scenes of the young Caroline (played by Meghann Fahy) and her husband, "but nobody ever had a better one. It lasted a year to the day... I knew that if he had the courage to risk dying I had to have the courage to risk living."

Caroline was pregnant when he left. As the train pulls away, she realizes she forgot to give him her valentine card. She runs to him and after a passionate last-kiss hands him her card. He opens the red envelope to find a hand-made heart which reads, "Now you have my heart. Keep it next to yours and bring it back to me." His letters come regularly at first but one day she gets the hated telegram "M.I.A." – Missing in Action. She's never able to find out what happened to him. The journalist Susan initially got interested in the story because she wanted to understand what made someone like Caroline stay committed all these years. She was on the fence about accepting a proposal from someone who was never there for her. As she got to know Caroline she became attached to her entire family and particularly Caroline's grandson Lucas Thomas (played by Sean Faris). She told Lucas, "This isn't a heart break. She just never gave up on love."

Susan set out to find out what she could about Neil, using all her connections. Following an interview with a Senator she asks for his help and gets some information. She updates Lucas about another fellow who was with Neil at the end and had returned home, "Unfortunately, there was a little paperwork snafu, and he was officially classified as killed in the line of duty, until seven years ago, when he actually died of natural causes, as the paperwork got straightened out. And I'm guessing that your grandmother had stopped looking by then." And Lucas says, "Not to mention, it was probably a little late for him to tell us anything really useful." But Susan is determined, "Dead men talk all the time Lucas." Indeed they do. She learns that Neil had died heroically, sacrificing his life to save others. The military returned his remains and finally recognized him, "For meritorious conduct in the face of the enemy and for gallantry above and beyond the call of duty, Lieutenant Neil Thomas, United States Navy, will be posthumously awarded a Purple Heart, the Silver Star and the Navy Cross." Caroline was waiting for him at the railroad station when he returned. The valentine heart she wanted him to bring back and the photo of the young Caroline with their child were in his wallet. "I don't believe in giving up on things," she told Lucas when he wanted to dig up the "dried-up" rosebush that she and Neil had planted years ago.

Nowadays, there are fewer than half-a-dozen days in the year considered special and worthy of celebration but when I was young there were plenty. My life has been enriched by festivities and traditions which were sacrosanct at one time but have since vanished or been extinguished. Every season of my childhood was blessed by a procession of saints, each one demanding adoration and decoration. It was the job of a patron saint to guard and protect its town-people. It was the devotion of mere peasants that elevated a meagre existence into a heavenly odyssey. Preparations were made for the celebration weeks in advance. Young ladies would sew themselves a new skirt for the occasion. Savoury dishes and delectable sweets were prepared. Some baked creations were beautiful masterpieces that no one dare break or sample before or after the celebration. It felt sinful to eat them.

On the feast of the venerated saint, a statue would be paraded through the town for adoration. The heavy monument would be balanced on a platform and carried on wooden poles by rows of devotees (mostly men). The route of the procession would be transformed. The cobblestone pavement would be lined with flower petals. Balconies were embellished. Some devotees awaited a blessing or a miracle. They had paid a penance or promised an offering in exchange. Their house entrance would display their deep devotion. Hand-embroidered lace would showcase super-sized cookies braided and beaded and decorated fancifully. The devotee hoped their sacrifice would please and satisfy the saint and demonstrate they were deserving of the blessings. Sometimes the priest would enter their house and bless the home and family with holy water. The worshippers would follow behind the statue praying, chanting, and singing loudly for the saint to hear. Devotees would rush to the statue to kiss a foot or a hand, and to make an offering ("dono" in donation means gift). The celebration would continue into the night. Fireworks would light up the sky in the evening and a live band would fill the night with music and song, so loud as to be heard from the heavens.

Most of us have abandoned the practice of worshipping statues and baking fanciful idols but that doesn't mean that we are better off.

It is essential that we replace by-gone traditions with new ones, no matter how lame they may seem. We have to intentionally string pearls of joy together one at a time. Setting the table with our best china for a Sunday brunch makes our family feel like guests. Getting all dolled up and spending a romantic evening with a partner rekindles our passion. Masquerading with good friends on Halloween is a lot of fun. Toasting the end of every grade with your child is a confidence boost. Decorating the house every Christmas with children's crafts, lights, and pine cones puts another nostalgic memory in our album of favorite snapshots. This is how we infuse our lives and that of our loved ones with fond memories and create traditions. It's well worth the effort.

40 | LIVE, LAUGH, AND JUST BE.

"Catch the Spark Within" is about being fully alive. There is both pain and joy in living. Being sad or happy is a state of mind. It is a way of reflecting on our circumstances. We cannot be happy every minute of the day just as we cannot be sad for always. The goal is to live, laugh, and just be. Happiness and sadness will follow. The way we process life makes all the difference. A gratitude journal can help. It makes the best rise to the surface. Laughter and beauty exalt the spirit. It's all good.

Most of us think that we have to be successful to be happy. Only then, will we be fulfilled. If that were the case, our world would be a happier place. After all, we have achieved so much as a human race. Even more astounding, is how much has been achieved during our lifetime. While success trumps failure in sparking feelings of satisfaction, success gives our lives only surface shine. All glory is fleeting. We have to feel whole to be truly fulfilled. We have to make peace with ourselves to feel whole.

Becoming whole requires that we heal those wounds in us that we don't even know are there until we feel the pain. It's a process. It is only by embracing all the parts that we become whole. We have to cry when it hurts. We have to laugh at ourselves. We have to play and have fun. Other actors can play a role in mending us but they are only a supporting cast. We have the lead role. Life is not a rehearsal. Every day is a live performance. We have to live gratefully, laugh often, and just be.

"Tweet...Tweet" is an immersion course in life. We can't get whole by dipping only one foot in the water. We have to jump in with both feet no matter what. We have to feel the heat and the cold to become whole. Eventually we get peaceful. We feel content. When we feel content we can do anything. When we feel whole, we are open to new possibilities. Everything is as it should be. Live, laugh, and just be.

REFERENCES & QUOTATIONS

A Thousand Words – comedy drama film (2011): Directed by Brian Robbins; with Eddie Murphy   2, 46

Arianna Huffington – Great Conversations #302 with Howard Fineman 4, 13

August Rush – romantic musical film (2007): Directed by Kirsten Sheridan; with Freddie Highmore, Keri Russell, Jonathan Rhys Meyers, and William Sadler 42, 45

Black Gold – adventure drama film (2011): Directed by Jean-Jacques Annaud; with Freida Pinto, Mark Strong, Antonio Banderas, and Tahar Rahim 2

Break Lyrics – Steve Erlody and Jonathan Rhys Meyers (2007); Sung by Jonathan Rhys Meyers in film "August Rush"   49

Burlesque – romantic musical film (2010): Directed by Steve Antin; with Cher, Christina Aguilera, Cam Gigandet, and Stanley Tucci 19

Cast Away – romantic drama film (2000): Directed by Robert Zemeckis; with Tom Hanks, Helen Hunt, Paul Sanchez, and Lari White   48

Charlie St. Cloud – romantic drama film (2010): Directed by Burr Steers; with Zac Efron, Amanda Crew, and Charlie Tahan   7

Easy A – teen comedy film (2010): Directed by Will Gluck; with Emma Stone, Amanda Bynes, Cam Gigandet, Dan Byrd, Lisa Kudrow, and Patricia Clarkson   17

Ross; with Jennifer Lawrence, Josh Hutcherson, Wes Bentley, Stanley Tucci, Woody Harrelson, and Willow Shields 12

Casual reference to, and quotations from some of my favourite people: Oprah Winfrey, Dr. Oz, Dr. Phil, Anderson Cooper and other sages and artists.

ABOUT THE AUTHOR

Alex Abaz is a passionate and purposeful woman that loves innovative projects. She is a hardcore entrepreneur that has built companies from the ground up. Not only does she love to color outside the lines, her work spills out of the box.

The 2007 film, "P.S. I Love You" says it best for Alex. When Holly first meets Jerry she tries to impress him with her grand plans and ends up quoting William Blake, "I must create... my business is to create... or be enslaved by another man's ...something." She explains, "Just create something new and there it is. And it's you out in the world outside of you... And you can look at it, or hear it, or read it, or feel it...and you know a little bit more about you. A little bit more than anybody else does."

It's not unusual for Alex to have several projects on the go. She is presently working on some new titles in different categories and a couple of websites. You can reach Alex at so.o.good.shop@gmail.com.

OTHER BOOKS BY ALEX ABAZ

Inside the Polar Vortex of an Arctic Winter Blast: Collection of photographs and inspirational verses

The Go-to Book on google+: Marketing through Social Media

Cut to the Chase! The best sites to learn how to build & sell online

Vivere: Live, Laugh & Just Be!

Download a digital copy from Publish Digitally at
https://sites.google.com/site/publishdigitally/

Or visit Amazon at https://www.amazon.com/author/alex_abaz

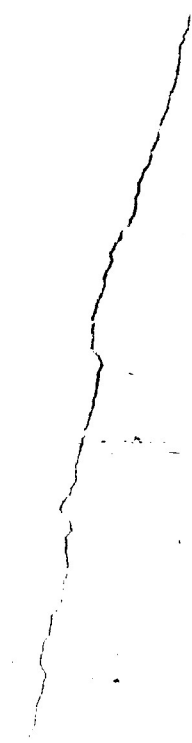